Terrorism, Ethics, and Modern Society

Terrorism, Ethics, and Modern Society

Lawrance George Lux

Writers Club Press

San Jose New York Lincoln Shanghai

Terrorism, Ethics, and Modern Society

Writers Club Press
an imprint of iUniverse, Inc.

For information address:
iUniverse, Inc.
5220 S. 16th St., Suite 200
Lincoln, NE 68512
www.iuniverse.com

ISBN: 0-595-21270-0

Printed in the United States of America

For all the dead, who died needlessly.

Contents

Foreword

The United States began the economic process of Standardization of Parts in the American Civil War to increase war production of vital materials. This process spread throughout the American economy rapidly, taking firm hold by the end of the War. The Concept spread to Europe within a decade. The spread of Ideas was rapid when such Ideas held great benefit, even in a Time and Age where Letters took an average month to deliver. The dissemination of Information did not hold the same consistency where there was not the common perception of benefit. Many ideas first expressed in this Period have yet to complete the journey of passage to common understanding. Transference primarily occurred if the messengers held awareness of the personal benefits to be derived.

Two factors remain incisive in the transmutation of Ideas to general knowledge; the level of Education of the Transmitters, and their occupational specialization. Insufficient educational levels would derive little understanding of value in the Idea, with no personal interest if outside occupational usage. Great ideas of intrinsic value become lost in the dustbin of History, because of lack of receptive audience. The danger lurks especially for delineation of Moral Codes, normally termed as Ethics.

Discussion reaches critical mass in the World today, where production of almost any desired good can be accomplished cheaply, with ever-decreasing Resource devotion to the effort. The realm of Ethics has trailed far behind the capacity to enrich. Much outrage was exhibited less than twenty years ago when a High School student provided detailed plans for a nuclear bomb, capable of desired explosion along with cheap construction. The Author guarantees Someone will design a cheap nuclear reactor within a Generation, with the capacity to function in the environment of a house basement or Garage. We already possess an insidious Individual producing cheap Anthrax for distribution; with easy-access mailing lists off the Internet. He had been preceded by the Uni-bomber. Some impulse for the development of Moral Codes should be resident in the common Citizen today!

This Work hopes to be the first Shot fired, in a lengthy debate about Ethics and Modern Man. Conflict Resolution stays a constant topic throughout Academic discussions; yet, the Period since World War II is most noted for the lack of Conflict resolution. No Country has been forced to suspend It's aggressions permanently except for the Apartheid of South Africa, no guerilla movement has been completely terminated, and no issue of Territoriality had been resolved despite literally millions of man-hours of negotiation. The most remarkable feature of Conflict Resolution in the current World, continues to be a total lack of resolution. A different format of discussion needs to be initiated; and the installation of Ethics among all, provides the only likely avenue of success. The trouble lies in the fact no universal Ethical Code has ever achieved acceptance. We need to address this issue!

Lawrance George Lux

Preface

September 11, 2001 will predicate any serious intellectual discussion, until another vaster horror replaces It's image as the great Evil. The Author herein surrenders to the hypocrisy, and presents his own horror at the terrible wrong done to the Innocent Heros of New York, Pentagon, and Air passengers. There will be no reference to the more than Ten million peoples of the World, who died in mass murders committed since 1945. No mention made of the One Hundred Thousand plus killed and injured in Terrorists' attacks in over sixty-one Countries. Nothing said of the Two Million soldiers dead in the World from undeclared Wars since 1960. Unspoken will be the statement over Seven Hundred Thousand Murders were committed in the United States in the last Century. The Author will simply join the chorus, and condemn the despicable dastardly cowardice of the Terrorists of September 11.

The above may seem impious to those who may ever read the missive; yet, great stands the magnitude of Evil spawned by the unethically violent. Devotees of Conflict Resolution as a philosophy will proclaim the above events were caused by the inequities of modern life, split between the Haves and the Have-Nots. They make great mention of leveling the playing field, so all may benefit from the riches of modern society. This Mind-set will forever glow as a Utopian ideal, and will always remain a worthless ideal. Inadequacies of Education, occupational skills, resources, and Capital wealth dictate there will always be inequities. The World would find itself destitute of Resource, if even 25% of the World's population consumed resources at the rate of Americans. Education of the World's Illiterate to the level of American High School graduates would require 170 Million new teachers trained to the level of American College graduates, plus the investment of

Seven Trillion dollars in educational facilities. The occupational skills level of almost all of the World's population reaches as high, as their educational levels will allow. We will not find Salvation with platitudes.

1

Causes of Discordance

he Author seriously debated elimination of this Chapter, through fears of being thought eccentric and foolish; then decided Everyone considered him to be Insane anyway! He will try to be as logical as he can attain, in explanation of a World view considered essential to comprehension of the strife ever present. Those doubtful of the following discussion can move on to Chapter II; but will probably lack for some understanding of the Work.

A specific form of Reincarnation process appears overwhelmingly logical. Identities are known to be determined by DNA and RNA, which dictate not only physical characteristics; but also govern behavioral and emotional stabilities and mannerisms. Most Medical authorities would agree with the above statement as fully in accordance with current studies. An extrapolation of this statement offers the likely occurrence Genetics actually governs the nature of the environment, which the Organism finds itself in. This general statement must be broken down into more precise elements to establish validity.

Life defines as a journey from a point in the Past, to a point in the Future. The point in the Past can be defined as Initial Conception; the point in the Future defined as the point of Death. Medical authorities will assert the Individual holds definition by his Initial Conception, the matrix of DNA and RNA which determines what he is to be. They will also state this Initial Conception is exact; any conception of a different DNA and RNA matrix will develop a separate, distinct Individual or Organism. Logical sequence would dictate Reincarnation could occur if and only if each Initial Conception was an exact replication of the first Initial Conception defining the Individual. Any variation from the Initial Conception will lead to a different Organism.

The second Precept must be specific groups of DNA and RNA possess an affinity to each other. Medical authorities will quickly relate possible or impossible chance of parentage. One Individual could possibly give Initial Conception to another Individual, or he could not; simply by avenue of his own DNA and RNA matrix. This principle establishes the grounding expressed in social delineation of Family. Individuals could migrate from one family to another family; but only if the two families were of sufficiently close genetic structure to replicate the specific Individual. The limitation of possible families an Individual could be conceived within, establishes an outer parameter of potential environments an Individual could exist within.

Medical authorities will also advance the theory Individuals and Families consist genetically of extractions from others. Individuals are made up of parts of other Individuals; Initial Conceptions consist of DNA and RNA elements contributed by other Family members, while body construction differentiation comes from DNA and RNA elements coming from outside the Family circle. This theory, though understood with acceptant reservation by the Medical Geneticists, has almost no acknowledgment in literature. Food and drink are the expected transference mechanism of the later DNA and RNA elements. There is belief such later transference governs the potential children which an Individual could conceive. The Author feels the point of separation between Family-supplied genetic material, and outside genetic material, comes with puberty; Family genetic material controlling childhood development.

Individuals, under this theoretical analysis, become Units initially composed of elements of their families; and later to be developed by an outer environment. Families become basic affinities tied to each other, but with extension throughout a greater environment. Individual Organisms survive because of affinities to their families plus outside support. Families attain their support and strength through the multiple associations or interactions with the outer environment. Such theory still lacks debate, and suffers from a shortage of research on the actual genetic relationships along with their potential formation. This discussion will progress as if the theory was proven fact.

The actual physical process of Living places an ongoing stress on the Individual organism; reflected as an Aging process. A more explorative definition could be the longer a given structure has been existent, the greater the accumulative impact or weathering has been endured. Affinity of Genetic materials cannot permanently endure constant, accumulative stress; the association is weakened by multiple events pulling in spreading directions. This may or may not be a relevant observation. It is known Aging and It's effect remains a programable process; which the Medical profession tries to delay, though it cannot be stopped or reversed. The Author stands firm in the conviction that Aging, or the sustained accumulative stress, provides the entire structure for History; the process unstoppable and irreversible, precluding any return to the Past as a viable social forum.

A base foundation has been established through which Reincarnation could possibly take place. The Individual could possibly be reincarnated by any family with sufficient genetic affinity to serve as had his original family. The number of reincarnations possible would depend upon the number of families with the ability to contain his Initial Conception. The impulse for those secondary conceptions would be the Individual's association with the outside environment in his adult development. This impulse would reduce under the stress of Aging on the outer environment, causing alterations of those associations. The families, themselves, would develop differing affinities of genetic material as the Individuals composing the initial family left; supplanted by new family members.

Reversion to the original discussion elicits the repeated statement Individuals must be conceived as they were initially, to be themselves. This makes the Individual the permanent stability, and the Family the instrument of change. The Individual migrates through families currently capable of conceiving him; until he has migrated through all such families, possibly extended because of the development of new affinity genetic families. The outer environment will hold tight to the Individual, until living stress separates such associations. The Author believes this later living stress separation provides for the conception of animals.

The conception of animals comes from partial loss of family affinity, with continued impulse by the outer environment for conception of the Individual. The partial conception derived leads to an animal form being conceived, because the entirety of the initial conception was not present. Conceptions will continue, even though they are only partial conceptions; until Aging stress eliminates the association of adult life. The fate of the Individual is to regress to earlier Periods of time with what part of Himself is still human, living the human life of those times of which he is still capable. His outer form in the Present is that of the animal conceived. This process will continue until the point when all human associations have been stressed by Age into separation. An alternate explanation could be his entire human life has been lived, and he is absolute dead.

The outer environment formation, likewise development of primordial emotional surges, finds possible generation through the above-stated theory. Both family-affinity and outer environment genetic relationships may fall into a classification system based upon the exact familiarity of one Individual to another. The range of classification could range from immediate family intimates, distant family relations, friends, neighbors, work associates, common citizenry, foreigners, strangers, various classes of animals, various classes of Plants, and finishing with various classes of materials to the final end of the ground We walk upon. Each level of classification may exhibit it's own emotive response in the Individual organism; each governed by the degree of danger to the association and importance of the association. The Reader should remember this stands only as speculation on the composition of World structure; as believed by a Man, who never claimed to be a Genius.

The above theory, if true, brings illumination to the difficulties of human conflict resolution. Descent into greater distance in any association does not automatically lessen the importance of association. It may be an extreme distance from Individual to the ground he walks upon in terms of intimacy; yet, he must have firm foundation and place on which to grow food. Animal and Plant species are much the same; still, they are the source of food. Other materials, though as distant in association as the ground, provide the form of his home, vehicles, and equipment to earn his livelihood. Intimate distance possesses no relevance to the importance of association. Distance does lessen the human interplay associated in the relationship. The progression proceeds from human love and friendship, to distant human recognition, to animal recognition, to end in simple appearance of the Corpse. Each level distancing eliminates another intrinsic element of humanity, until none remains; though the importance of relation may not reduce at all. Emotive reaction may become quite violent, where importance of association sustains, but human feeling has descended to the Beast.

Clear observance witnesses the ease with which Children accommodate differences amongst themselves; later Adults, even the same Individuals as the Children noted above, often reach an impasse where no concessions will be made. The intransigency could possibly be defined by the above analysis. The Children, close in human association, are distant from their adult associations; allowing for human feelings to determine conflict resolutions. Adults, on the other hand, possess a greater multiplex of associations, with far less human association involved in the greater majority. The non-human associational interplay dictates adamant stands, based on necessity fulfilment of non-human desires.

A final point to the theory advanced must be the classification of levels of distance hold relevance only in the human social context as separation by Generations. They possess the only textual affinity to distance classifications, and more research may indicate Generations and levels of distance equate to be one and the same. This brings forth further speculation. Each Adult Individual establishes his own associations with the outer environment. Equation of Generation as distance association stipulates an ever-expanding involvement with the outer environment, as each level of distance generates it's own periphery of association.

Investigation of the phenomena would suggest Age of the Individual exhibits an almost universal association with the outer environment; curtailing attempts to eliminate the Individual from society, unless the Individual expresses absolute incompetence to perform in that society. It is not saying the Individual cannot be killed. It simply details overwhelming pressure for Reincarnation of the Individual; as exact replica, or as partial identity animal. The outer environment would and could not withstand the degree of loss in association. Individuals possessing greater Age express greater survivability, and greater potentiality for Reincarnation.

Review of the material leads immediately into a discussion of Criminality. It has been proclaimed living stress (Aging) is accumulative and irreversible previously in the discussion. It is now asserted Criminality is simply attempts to reverse the Aging process, at least the loss of power from loss of association. Individuals, in their totality or complete complex of associations, perceive the accumulative effect of living stress as a loss of personal power. Simpler put: They see themselves of descending from of a position of Great Chief, to the level of Little Indian. They search for means to stop and reverse this digression.

The means by which such attempts are made require examination. Only one method appears to the Author which could account for Criminality, and recreate lost personal power. This process consists of convincing Children the distant level of association is much more intimate, than generational level would dictate. The Criminal does assure the Child of much greater personal power, if the Child would take additional material from himself; and work much harder for the Criminal, than the level of association would decree. The Whole of the process is perversion of the actual Life process. The Criminal is actually the only one to benefit; he has the work he should be doing done by the Child, while he enjoys the enrichment from the exercise, being paid for the labor. The Child does not receive payment for the effort, suffers from a form of Insanity through seeing what are basically animal images, and exhausts his own energies-a process actually aging the Child faster than ordinary living stress would dictate. The Criminal uses the enrichment of himself from the efforts of the Child, to subvert further Children into perversion; and destroy enemies-enemies defined as any who produce heavy living stress upon himself.

The concept of a Criminal's enemies must be further explored. Intense study of the identity of such enemies would indicate probable identity as those who should have adult association with the Child being perverted by the Criminal. Their attempts to establish normal association with the Child brings intense pressure on the Criminal. The Criminal's destruction of these Individuals using the resources generated by the efforts of the Child, actually reduce the Child's ability to survive and organize a life of his own. A Child who comes to understand the destruction of the Criminal and begins to fight his dominance; finds the Criminal uses the subordination of other children suborned through the Child's efforts, to destroy the Child himself. The Criminal can therefore be defined as a malignant parasite destructive to everyone; but greatest to the host Child themselves.

It is now time to relate Terrorist to Criminal. The Terrorist remains nothing more than a Criminal who has lost the support of the Children, whom have recognized his malignant nature. The Terrorist threatens the Children through the process of threat; said threat to dump upon them the destroyed enemies of the Criminal, who are actually the adult associations the Children would normally of had if the Criminal had not destroyed them. The Children actually require rebuilding of such Individuals, to reconstruct their own lives. The Terrorist uses his actual distance level from the Children, and the extended resources he has from the Children's efforts, to apply great pressure on the Children; preventing such reconstruction. The Children must call upon their family-affinity associations, and the surviving Adult associations; in order to rebuild the adult associations destroyed by the Criminal. The Children are either killed, or aged more than they should be by the high living stress. The Terrorist loses in any case, as he has lost the ability to suborn more Children into perversion. The increased living stress of his activities will bring about his demise.

It reveals to this Author Terrorist activities, plus the Criminal activity which spawns it, consist of only a temporary anomaly in the lifetime of individual organisms; yet, such activities can consume levels of personal and social resources, of magnitude to seriously depress the standard of living of the specific Individual and the greater society. It retards the development of Civilization through wastage. The advantages of Education and technology lost, because of response of Children to Criminal identities. Reversion to bestial patterns of social behavior produce damage to both the Individual, and the structure of Society.

Great difficulties ensue as the Individual and Society try to stop the incursion of Terrorism and Criminality. Western societies cherish a long history of limitation of Governmental power to violate the integrity of the Individual; they also have a much shorter history of actual personal liberty. Almost all educated elites in these Western societies will dramatically oppose any shrinkage of Individual civil rights. This Author is not a Hobbes-ian, and he would join those ranks. There remains an absolute refusal to tear apart society, simply to rebuild society correctly. Options of reducing Civil rights would fail to accomplish the task anyway; confronted with numerous obstructions advanced later. These restrictions of Governmental investigation and operations nevertheless constitute a real impotence factor for Government action. There are many others to be contested.

A real barrier to the transmission of Knowledge comes by avenue of Generation Gap; each Generation governed by a personal matrix maturation, particular to that Generation. The pattern of Events occurrence in the growth span of every Generation sets the attitude for the greatest majority in the Generation. The same language may be spoken by all Generations; but different weights are applied to the Words, due to Generational attitude. Few Spokespersons for every Generational attitude provide a coherent consistency, until somewhere in mid-life when educated elites think to justify their personal life choices (consider the current effort by the Author). This mutual incoherence between Generations leads to varying degrees of support for any social action. The factor becomes aggravated by personal corruption, with the ranks of Criminals increasing in every Generation with the aging of the group.

Another disastrous restraint on action against the malignant forces in society lies in the production of puberty. Children traditionally alienate from their Parents at this stage; confronted by hormonal processes which incite Parents to often adopt the trappings of a Police force. Children learn warily discussion of life daily events bring on criticism, with insistent proposals of personal behavior which would make the Children the butt of ridicule by their contemporaries. Children quickly adopt the Party line developed by their own Generation, designed to placate Parents, avoid censure, and free from restrictions. A sub-society is created with it's own formal language, and it's own personal interpretation of the language. The threat of Parental action is removed; but so is effective communication.

The Conflict between Young and Old also enters the Picture, with real divergence of interests. The Young feel victimized by the wealth and privilege of the Old. The Old cite the privilege and wealth be the product of hard labor, and insist the Young imitate the cited hard labor. The Young witness the real fact of the Old not actually working as hard as they claim; perceiving the largesse of the Old's wealth and privilege comes in most part to a 'Good Old Boy' network of associations. The Young study the hypocrisies of the statements of the Old, and doubt seriously hard work had been the venue of the Old's wealth and privilege. The Young also spot the levels of corruption exhibited in those associations, and estimate such corruption was the source of the wealth and privilege.

The Young understand another clear aspect of the activities of the Old and their associations, which is a very real attempt to personally profit from the hard work of the Young. The Young feel cheated by the Old, and even older Criminally-minded sympathize with the Young; claiming they were equally victimized by the Old. The Criminal promises the Young their rightful due, if the Young helps the Criminal destroy the associations of the Old. The foundation of a War between Age groups has been outlined; the Criminal as allies, and the Old and their associations as enemies. Attempts by the Old to limit the destruction of Criminality is understood by the Young as attack made upon their own associations, the outlet through which they hope to attain wealth and privilege for themselves.

The drift between Generations now becomes clear! An actual battle-ground environment has developed; the Young's perception of Adult movement against Criminality being an attack upon their own associations, their chosen path to attain wealth and power. The Young begin to protect the Criminal from Adult persecution. They begin to hide evidence and location of Criminals. They organize an institutional condemnation of snitching, the practice of providing information on Criminal activities to law enforcement agents. They start to imitate the Criminal supported, and turn violent against those who would break the associations. The Young are corrupted where they have adopted the Criminal mentality, and attack the Innocent. The outrage of the Old towards this behavior is seen by the Young only as enemy propaganda, designed to destroy themselves and their allies.

The humor probably apparent only to the Author; but all such activities require hard work on the part of the Young, work which the Criminal is not able to do. The work makes the Young a difficult host for the Criminal, to the point the Criminal must turn Terrorist in order to control the Young. The Young start to mature because of the efforts they are putting in; both in support of the Criminal perceived as ally, and in the work demanded of them by the Old. Clarity of mind finally convinces the Young working legitimately provides greater, and more consistent, pay; than anything derived from the Criminal, which likely remains nil. The Young redirect their efforts to exploitation of legitimate occupation, and so has become the enemy of the Criminal; who now seeks the destruction of the Young.

A Terrorist remains nothing more than a Criminal who have lost the opportunity to suborn more Children, due solely to lack of reach based on absence of power. The Terrorist turns to organizations of his own Generation, which survive into the Present Generation. He chooses those specific organizations which exhibit a megalomania (i.e., an inherent right to rule; in other words, a religion or aristocratic institutions), and the Terrorist organizes a Cult whose membership consists of Individuals who thirst for power. The Terrorists instruct Cult membership to solicit funding from family members and membership of the religion of which they are affiliated. The Terrorists' proclaimed occupation becomes the destruction of the power of ruling elites for their funding Contributors. The Terrorist enjoys the ability to threaten, by his potential ability to destroy Children; who had previously supported the Terrorist, before maturing to the point where the Terrorist could not control the Child.

The Terrorist cannot survive, because he cannot handle the living stress of the modern age; he lacks the skills and resources for legitimate employment in society, at least at the occupational levels he would desire. His ability to corrupt the Young has failed, because of lack of personal resource and reach. He cannot control previously suborned Children. His remaining source of funding will fail as his ineffectuality becomes common knowledge. He will not survive, or will his personal agenda. The sole problem lies with the support he derives from megalomanic institutions; themselves destined to fail, but of presently wide popular support. The Terrorist can use this support to destroy the Children, who had previously supported the Terrorist. Megalomaniacal institutions grant the Terrorist the power to destroy! They grant this power because of personal institutional desire to rule; they fail because of lack of support for demands for what is basically Slavery. The combination of the two, Terrorist and Megalomanic, bring destruction to anyone; who had previously supported them,, unless stopped by the total order of the Greater Society.

2

Breaking the Chain of Criminality

The above analysis propels for re-education of the Young; but such training suffers from serious considerations. Parent and Educator endure the alienation of Generation Gap, and representation as an Oppressor class. Social conditions encourage corruption; and actually retard success of ethical behavior. The activities of their Elders provide the Young with justification for their own corrupt behavior. Ethical practices will never be instilled into the Young, unless the Old break from their favorable positions of advantage to the degree the Young can understand common procedures apply to all. The entire society must move to ethical standards, else education of the Young in proper conduct will fail.

The Young must come to realize they can succeed within the system of their Parents, until such time as they acquire the system to do as they wish. This means discrimination against the Young for enrichment of the older Generation must cease. The upshot must be the caste of privilege destroyed! This caste stands as a powerful element in modern society, and immediately works for it's own self-preservation. The entirety of society must join in elimination of the caste of privilege, else the Reformers fail. Reform will call for a partnership with the Press to guarantee such Public support.

Any Study must advance concrete proposals; otherwise, the investigation serves only to confuse and mislead. Public readers can only support that which is understood and accepted; clear guidelines alone serve the purpose. Later Chapters will give ethical grounding to many of the proposals herein proposed; but hopefully, an innate awareness will quickly derive. Revision of the Tax Codes stand as the top priority to gain the support of the Young. Proper distribution of income alone will give the Young grasp of the Concept they can succeed in the system of their Parents. The new Tax Code must be fair, and show impartiality; and express immediate benefit for the Young. Placement of tax burden based upon privilege will forever alienate the Young; inciting them to turn to the Criminal. The question of how to revise the Tax codes become the Issue.

A Property Holders Tax Code should be implemented. The general outlines of this Tax Code says there should be graduated Income Tax paid by Everyone, without exception. Tax Rates should be Ten percent on the first $20,000 dollars of taxable Income, with a Two percent rise in tax rate for every additional $20,000 of Income ad infinitum. There will be absolutely no deductions of any kind; Business and Corporation only allowed to deduct accepted expenses. There is one and only one Investment credit: the ability to deduct Twenty percent of the tax burden, if new Investment can be proven. Income will be considered as Income, not matter the source-Capital gains, royalties, rents, interest, or wages; the unified Tax Code will govern all Income increments, without examination of manner derived.

The above Tax Code alone will not bring the support of the Young. Their belief in the system will come only with concern for their situation. The Tax Code should carry the stipulation the tax burden will be collected from all without reservation; but those who can prove a capital-accumulation less debt of less than $30,000 will have the entirety of the tax burden placed in the Individual's name at a Mutual Fund of their own choice. This option does not apply to Business or Corporation. The Young will grasp the taxation goes to their immediate benefit, in order to ensure the development of their personal financial position. The provision will also provide a reconstruction base for all suffering from bankruptcy. Direct incentive will be induced for the Poor to work.

The Economist in the Author states the real tax burden will resemble the stipulated tax rates, and provide ample revenues to a judicious Government structure. Graduated tax rate increases for Business and Corporation will cease after a Forty percent tax rate has been reached; for the simple reason all would benefit from business promotion. Tax evasion will prove almost impossible without the commission of perjury. The tax base will be sufficiently wide, the loss of income through transmission to the Young goes unnoticed. Social Security and Government transfer payments become taxable, but without loss; unless the Taxpayer has too great a capital accumulation. Medicare payments are also taxable, but excused if a Taxpayer would result in a capital accumulation loss to less than $30,000. Medical, Life, and Property Insurance payments will be considered as repayments of previous loans (premiums). All of the tax base would realize they have opportunity to acquire a capital base.

The next attempt to woo the Young away from the Criminal comes in the manner of law enforcement. The Legal Code today stands as an entombed dinosaur of a pastoral age. The allotments of Sentence to Violators stands as an overpowering joke. Judges exhibit childish concerns when They should be dispensing adequate justice. The entire concept of the Legal Code must be altered. The punitive nature of the Code should be discarded; possessing opposition to it's imposition-especially in the placement of Death Sentences. A more sensible Legal Code must come into play.

A most notable possible Legal Code is the Real Damage Legal Code. The Real Damage Legal Code establishes a monetary price for each and every offense. Damage to Property will be equated to the cost of reconstruction. Theft will be the actual dollar loss, or the actual insurable value of said property. Assault would be assessed all medical bills plus lost income. Murder would be assessed as the total earned income of the Individual in his lifetime-never less than One Hundred Thousand to protect children. Rape and Child Abuse will be assessed all medical costs, all lost income, and all potential lost income due to emotional distress (never more than $100,000). The Court assumed the payment of claims to the victims, and sets the Violator's sentence to the amount of work necessary to repay the Court. The Penal system will be charged to provide all employment consistent with repayment of the Court; the Violator charged by the Penal system for board and room. The Violator will not be eligible for Parole until at least Twenty percent of the debt is discharged, and is liable for repayment of the entire amount whether imprisoned or not; this debt cannot be set aside by bankruptcy proceedings. Prisoners who refuse to work will be confined what is commonly referred to as the 'Hole', and given only a twice-daily bland diet without taste. Any failure to make debt repayments to the Court will induce automatic revocation of Parole.

The Real Damage Legal Code serves multiple purposes. It sets the length of Sentence for Violations in most Cases. It allows for the proper adjudication of Parole. It dismisses the possibility of Probation, which is simple nullification of punishment for legal offense. White Collar criminals face the same punishment structure as lower-class criminals. A Bank Robber who manages to steal $400 from a Teller, will not do the fifteen years given to a Bank Robber who steal Five million dollars. The major drug dealers will be fined an amount totaling the total value of illegal drugs distributed by the Individual; who will serve a much longer sentence than a Street corner dealer. Embezzlers and Con-artists will repay the total amount of their theft plus damages. High-priced, high-powered lawyers will not save the Criminal any longer with plea-bargained slap on the wrist. The Death Sentence can be retained for bestial crimes and acts of Mass Murder.

The great value of Real Damages Sentencing for Criminal behavior resides in the end-deterrence of such behavior. Quickly understood will be the knowledge punishment is meted out according to injury, and the fact such punishments are accumulative; Crime will not pay, no matter the frequency of repetition. Any Criminal understands it matters not if they are only caught once out of fifteen times a Crime is committed; a sequence of captures leads to a permanent life sentence. Children will come to realize the Criminal as a self-made Slave; who lacks romance, or the ability to fend off Society. Crime becomes a trap, which ruins life's choices.

The orientation of Educational efforts must be altered, to induce personal responsibility in the Student. The gist of current American Educational applications attempts to force-feed the child, without his outward notice. The Child derives no real awareness of the process, until confronted by a lack of success. Instructors try to make the process completely painless and success-motivational; simply negating the value of the Education. The Child never comprehends the uniqueness and utility of the experience. He leaves the educational forum, to be confronted by a harsh World; interested only in goal attainment, with little concern for the laborer. The Child-adult finds himself in a Prison of insensate demands, without the help on which he has become dependent.

The incidence of Office-worker assaults upon their co-workers are the direct result of the above-mentioned Educational methods. The Workplace demands a certain schedule of accomplishment; set not at the level of the Individual's aptitude, but on the needs of the overall production level. The laborer finds his co-workers overburdened with their own duties, and undesirous of extended provision of supervision and aid to others. Co-workers will not take the place of Teachers as in the educational system. The acculturated Individual from the educational system cannot work at his own pace like before, and finds his co-workers will not act as guardian angels for someone who cannot maintain the pace demanded. Sharp rebuke from co-workers feeds a resentment, already large because of the persistent demands placed upon the Individual. Co-workers become an object of hatred, because they will not baby the Individual. The laborer, spoiled by the educational system, feels justified in responding with violence.

What directions could Education take in order to lessen the corruption of young labor assets? Policies should be implemented pushing the student into development of self-discipline. The statement remains much easier to dictate, than it is to initiate. An embedded bureaucracy lives within the Educational Establishment, backed by a huge list of Educational professionals; who made their reputation on institution of current educational practices. They are backed by a horde of Parents, who must listen to the pleas of their children; who are not concerned by their final development, only the degree of hardship they have to face. A Policy which suggests an increase of student responsibility will immediately be declared as Draconian. The well-being of Society becomes the last concern. Consider the demise of bi-lingual education; teachers still refuse to abide by confining education to English, though English language capacity is mandatory for the American workplace.

The discussion hereafter becomes quite controversial, because of the attack upon cherished beliefs. The first assault must be insistence on a specific uniform dress. The Author would go much farther than predecessors; stipulating a specific uniform for both boys and girls, specifically purchased from School-sponsored Venders. The uniforms defined as standard in quality, and undifferentiated in style. The children will not be allowed to differentiate based on family income or social position. The use of jewelry, make-up, and hairstyle will be limited, and subject to standards. It must be re-emphasized to the children repeatedly: differentiation must come only through academic achievement, or success in School activities. The Child comes to integrate the Concept of Marketplace demands.

The normal grading system of Today's schools must be discarded for a greater Workplace evaluation of Success. All Educational classes must be broken into gradable segments of approximately one Week's duration. Such segments must be graded according to a statistical base. A Student's advance in Grade level must be predicated by a certain average of all segments of say Seventy percent or better. A Counselor must discuss the student's segments with the Student every year. The segments will be designed to haunt the Student; they will be a permanent element of his educational record. He will be allowed to retest any segment desired at a later specified time each year he is in the School system; hoping to attain a higher statistical segment score. The Counselor must assure the Student that low segment scores will detract from Employers hiring practices in later years. The Student comprehends he must learn that which he ignored, or failed to learn previously. Students acquire the knowledge failure will not dissipate, or become lost in the shuffle.

The educational system comes to imitate the Workplace for the Student; inadequate performance will have to be redone, else the failure becomes a permanent mark with financial consequences. Individual failure on first effort will not be aided in succeeding attempts. A correspondent example from the Workplace is the passage of Legal Boards to practice Law in a State. Vast effort and funds went into a law degree, but no one will help any one who failed the Legal Boards on first attempt; the Individual must prove his ability to practice Law. The Student in the educational system will be faced with the same system; and an innate understanding what he misses on the first learning session, he must learn for himself or fail. The educational system will not relate how many times a Student had to test for a segment score of high value, only release final scores. The system which the Student must endure provides the propellent to learn, forcing a self-discipline of hard study; before consistent failure incites needs for enjoined hard effort.

The role of Sports need be reviewed by Educators. It has always been reiterated Sports are excellent for character development, by teaching the principles of Group effort and Team success. This thesis must be reviewed! Sports teach the application of intense efforts for the sole purpose of winning a Game, which will hardly be remembered once it is over. Athletes are taught by the endeavor to imitate Actors, to put on a huge production to entertain. They derive a shallowness of plan and action; defining their activity as inconsequential, forgotten and forgiven if substandard or poor. The Game becomes a simple entertainment, where huge effort is destined to come to naught, even if victory is attained. The athlete assimilate an ineffectuality to his effort, much like a mouse running on a wheel. This performance leads the athlete to assume his future behavior will have equally short-lived consequences.

The Author does not propound an end to athletics; a foolhardy wish in a Land in search of entertainment. He simply asserts such athletics should be attached to a long-range orientation, so the students learn a progression of effort. He would propose military training be integrated with High School activities. A normal School year with it's athletic activities should be followed by a summer of military training, graded like the above-mentioned segment grading system, and leading to more advanced military training through every year of High School. The serious purpose of such training would be constantly instilled in the Student body, and mandatory National Guard enrollment demanded for Six years after High School. The Student would find a occupational effort mandated after School, presenting continuity; and the serious needs of the Country served.

Children under a revised system of Education risk no more damage or threat, than currently endured by all in this Country. They would be pressured for success in their efforts, in a manner they would find later in the Workplace; eliminating the alienation which they now feel in the environment. The scope of Athletics will have changed; serving as the methodology of Group defense. Children could find proper challenge through grasp that proper expenditure of intellectual and physical effort must be utilized to provide their own individual performance for Group acceptance. They would come to realize each of them do make a difference, but only if they perform according to the needs of the Group. The effects of parental ineptitude ends in a continuous personal trial of performance, guided by Peer pressure and Authority.

The Japanese Educational system uses this responsibility placed on the Individual; their superior performance in the education of their Young shows it's effectiveness. The Japanese system fails in the protection of the Individual; Peer pressure is allowed too loose a rein. Society needs self-disciplined, responsible labor assets; not beaten Individuals cowering before their Peers. The institution of segment grading could force responsibility without Peer pressure, except in Group performance activities. These duties can be tightly defined and controlled by Authority-coach and military instructor. The individual student will recognize his acceptance and status depends upon adequate performance, as outlined by Authority.

All measures outlined in this Chapter labor for the integration of Youth into the larger Society, irrespective of Generation Gap and Generational cultures. The Young are propelled to work within the system, because adventures outside the system do not pay well and face ongoing censure. Immediate gratification of youthful desires allowed in a system which does not tarnish the gains of older Generations. Youth can easily define areas of opportunity open to them to fulfill their desires for advancement; while perceiving real restrictions in the violation of community goals. Individual image will be defined by greater Society goals, due to the labor effort demanded from them. Peer respect set by maintaining their own position in the common efforts of the Group.

We leave the arena of examination of Ourselves now, for the evaluation of Terrorists. We sought change in Ourselves, to kill the potential Terrorist within Our own populace; through opening up Society for all, especially the Young. We must first all share a liking and acceptance of Ourselves and each other, before We decapitate Terrorism. The drive for Profits and Gain in American society must be countered by a respect for others; the ground for this respect overwhelmingly sits on termination of all barriers to success, other than a personal achievement level .

3

The Mind of the Terrorist

The exact Profile of your average Terrorist remains unknown to the Author. Certain generative traits seem likely. Terrorists are split into two groups: those who devise and carry out exploitive attacks in urban centers, and the ones who infiltrate to snipe and bomb. The first Individuals assume a certain persona which does not help significantly to capture; but provides insight into their personality. They tend to be college-educated, coming from above-average income families in the Mid-East; never working to pay for their education or livelihood. Scholastic averages are likely above normal for these Individuals. Most seem to acquire the patina of a professional student; turning religious only at the point where family expectations push for actual work in an occupation. Religion comes to serve as the escape from personal responsibility, which Education had previously served. Most possess childhood records of violent behavior towards siblings, playmates, or animals (i.e. pets). Puberty often brings alienation from women, especially those who could be a sexual partner; often there are instances of un-returned love in the college years, rabid attitudes often expressed towards racial heritage of the spurning affection.

The turn to religion among this group often incurs a withdrawal from greater society, with intimate friendship with like-minded; often totally masculine groups with overtones of male homosexuality. Religious indoctrination inside the group does not follow the traditional Muslim pathway of general debate within the mosque. The college-oriented members of the Group derive the majority of religious thought from reading, with increasing tendency to pursue and debate more striated materials of radical religious leadership. Discussion remains confined to the Group, outside probable moderate dissent disallowed from entrance. Familial appeals and pressure for the Individuals to adopt occupation leads to radical expression among the Group. Such pressures commonly denounced as family corruption by Western values and culture. The individuals of the Group confront the necessity of joining the greater society as working elements, and opt to join the ranks of religious warriors in it's stead.

The Group turns to discussion of the methods of social disruption they should adopt. The Group will find an amazing amount of assistance in this endeavor. They find organizations who even provide training camps in the arts of Terrorist action. These organizations often demand tuition fees for attendance in seminars and training camps; but provide free seminars to such Groups on the methodology of requesting funds from their families, without giving the true rationale for the funds. Training from such organizations remain rudimentary, simply explaining the functioning of weaponry and construction of bombs. Attendance of these seminars and training camps brings indoctrination, which engenders dependance on the organizations; which are profit-motivated. The Group finds themselves buying weapons, explosives, false papers, and money transfers from such organizations with family funds.

The Group acquires a aura of suspense from such organizational training along with a sense of unstoppable mission. The organizations receive approximately one-third of their funding from such unknowing contributions of families of the Group members. The organizations instill in the Group the vital need for coordinated action; insisting the Group inform the organization of all proposed terrorist actions in advance. The Group is instructed to lay low otherwise; except for the practice of Group receipt of lists of soft Marks, from whom they are supposed to raise funds for the organization. This fund-raising becomes the mode of action for the Groups, spending late nights devising plans to destroy human beings in Group discussions. The organizations receive another one-third of their revenue from this fund-raising.

The organizations, informed of all proposals for Terrorist attack, have the essential controls in their hands. They can approve or disapprove all proposed attacks. It can precisely set the time of such attacks, and claim responsibility for such attacks; allowing for an increase in prestige and funding from trainees and contributors. The organizations are also allowed the privilege of another capability; the ability to inform on any Group. The ability to inform law enforcement agencies of impending terrorist action and planners, provides protection from criminal prosecution themselves, as a protected informant with reliable information. This capacity re-enforced by separation of the Groups, through proclaimed clandestine operation.

The Group becomes ever more radical and eager for demonstrative action with the increasing familial pressure for the Individuals of the Group to adopt gainful employment. Each Individual understands such action need be taken, before the source of livelihood dries up through family rejection. Gainful employment has assumed the mantle of a debasement of religious fervor; great excuse for embedded laziness. Plans for greater human destruction unfolds in Group discussions, demanding greater need for weapons, explosives, and false papers. The organizations sells such provisions with glee. It is also informed of intended operation. The organization examines the project; determining it's viability and possible threat to themselves from increased law enforcement pressure. Eighty percent of such plans turn into informant details for the organization's purchase of law enforcement protection. The Group finds it's way to prison, where they are freed from familial pressure and garnish rage against the greater society.

The organizations of Terror thrive as they are funded by families desirous of the children's education, said funds having been diverted for their own ends. The loss of a Group to prison means nothing to the organization, which gains more devoted Terrorists by the residence behind bars; families ready with funds to rehabilitate their children.

New recruits always available; noting the disdain of young ladies, turned off by obvious instability of suitors. Such organizations prove to be financially viable structures, much of Osama bin Ladin's fortune coming from the sale of weapons, explosives, training, and fund-raising.

Organizations of such order must possess a reputation to attract new recruits. They maintain this reputation by maintaining a para-military structure in some Country with a disturbed social environment. The Organization recruits on this home territory uneducated peasant lads, who they fill with religious fervor and zealot desire to destroy in the name of religion. The organization sends these fanatics without reflective structure out on suicidal missions. The success or failure of the suicide missions remain of prime importance. There must be a high failure rate, else the organization will find itself without martyrs or enemies. Either loss will bring a cancellation of the flow of funds to the organization from international source. It is often necessary to inform of prospective mission to insure freedom from loss of enemy potential. Failure assures credibility of claims for new recruits and greater financial backing.

The above analysis outlines the breeding ground for Terrorism; necessary components being a source of funding, a group of murderers willing to murder more gullible murderers, and a social environment willing to become inflamed by the mouthings of hatred. Also valuable to the equation becomes a substantial substandard religious leadership trained in the basic tenants of a religion once belligerent. The mullahs of Pakistan and Afghanistan are a prime example, but so is the Fundamentalist rabbis of Conservative Jewry. One can also mention the ministers of the Aryan Brotherhood and WASP Supremacists. Uneducated religious leadership may be defined as any ministry which condones, if not advocates, violence for any purpose, religious or otherwise. Such leadership gives Terrorism and it's organizations a canopy of rectitude, at least amid the less-educated of Congregations. Terrorist organization use such protection to defend themselves from the Moderates of the religion they proclaim as their own.

What is the message of hatred which all Terrorism proclaims, no matter of what origin? The primary claim resides in a message a powerful Enemy exists, who discriminates against those of your own origin. Al'Qaida claims it be Western nations, who enslave the Islamic peoples. Israelis scream out the hated PLO will destroy them. The PLO, itself, denounces World Jewry. Hindus howl against Muslims, with mutual response from Islam. White Supremacists wail Black people pollute the Aryan white race. Protestant and Catholic still kill in Northern Ireland, though they try to stop. Ethnic cleansing became the watchword in the Balkans. Communist dogma still kills in South America, while Parish priests still bless the growers of Cocaine. All groups claim some ministry as their Savior; all claim the Enemy as the incarnation of the Devil on Earth.

The third great tenant of Terrorism stands as the identification of the Enemy as Evil in total essence. This remains fundamental to the functioning of Terrorism. It strips individual responsibility from Terrorist action. The Enemy is Evil, in all of it's component parts; not leadership or class, but all of the Enemy. Man, Woman, Child makes no difference; all exist solely as component part of the Greater Evil. All can be attacked without conscience, because each and every one produces the Evil. The very identification of Evil sheds the right to fair play or defense. The Enemy can be attacked anywhere, in any form. The Terrorist finds justification in attacking the weakest and most incapable of defense. The Terrorist stands absolved of any individual responsibility for his conduct, as it was an assault against Evil. Murder in the greatest safety for the Terrorist guarantees protection on Earth, as well as in Heaven.

The identification of the Enemy as Evil serves another purpose as well; any defensive measure adopted by the Enemy is in itself Evil. The Enemy has lost irrevocably the right of self-defense. United States military action against bin Ladin and Taliban becomes unprovoked attack on the religious, because the Enemy deserves the massacre in New York; because of the Enemy's evil nature. Protection of the Faithful by all of the Faithful, no matter the criminal nature of the behavior of the Faithful. The Enemy loses both the right of Attack and Counterattack, simply because he has been defined as Evil. The Enemy retains only the right to be destroyed.

Most might conceive of the above as denouncement of Islam. Black men in the old South of the Ku Klux Klan faced lengthy imprisonment or hanging, for the defense against an assault from a White person. Criminal-driven Courts in the United States are still sentencing home-owners to prison, for having shot a burglar upon his entrance to the home. Hospitals treat some 19,000 Police officers per year, for injuries sustained by black assaults upon their persons; there are Six race riots per year on average, because of Police assaults on blacks. Ambulance response teams endure 1600 assaults per year on average; sixteen to twenty of such personnel are jailed every year, for carrying a concealed weapon. Thousands of Civilians are treated for injuries every year gen-erated by criminal attacks; Prosecutors will not prosecute such Cases, based solely on victim identification of the Assailant, even when the list of injuries has been extensive. A victim of a Crime cannot demand a jury trial of the Assailant, who can Plea-bargain a deal with insignifi-cant punishment; white collar Criminals the worst, who often get Community service after stealing Millions.

Discrimination flowers in modern society, and the Terrorist uses such discrimination for his own benefit. Passengers and Crew of Trans-port craft are prohibited from carrying self-defense mechanisms; mak-ing Terrorist attack both safe and effective. Foreign residents in the United States can purchase weaponry as easily as Citizens, without restriction. American Law prohibits only the carrying of a concealed weaponry; Police will still arrest a Civilian for carrying a loaded weapon in plain sight, as a Public danger. Americans in Islamic nations are not allowed to bring in a weapon, or purchase one; Islamic nations typically have instance of Natives carrying weapons which is Eight times the number carrying weapons in the United States. Explosives and Arms can be bought by natives of Islamic countries almost without Government restriction; the cost of such weapons, though, often limits purchase to funded Terrorists. Foreign Arms dealers can buy and sell weapons in the United States almost without restriction, if they are registered as an Arms dealer of some Nation with which the United States enjoys diplomatic relations.

The digression to ranting about the ineffectuality of American society to combat Terrorism will cease, with movement back to the mentality of the Terrorist. The Islamic Terrorist witnesses the freedom of Americans as religious violation, the Quar'on repeatedly stating the Infidel should be restrained from violation of laws of Allyah. This law refuses the right of a Woman to seek divorce, all Children belong to the father even if the father sought divorce; infidels cannot publicly preach their religious doctrines; infidels refused the right of Court petition against a member of the Faithful; infidels taxed a second measure above that paid by the Faithful; public exposure of Women-Faithful or infidel-forbidden; and injury to any of the Faithful should be the burden of all of the infidels with group punishment. Moderate Muslims claim such as ancient Islamic law is not currently in force; yet, it is exactly this law which the Islamic Fundamentalist and Terrorist would enforce.

The Terrorist absorbs this aspect of Islamic law, even if non-Muslim; the right to punish the entirety of a culture, for transgression of individual infidels. The only alteration to the text being in the definition of the infidels. The Terrorist claims group responsibility for the Enemy, yet proclaims sanctity for the Faithful; no matter what level of transgressions by individual Faithful. The Terrorist can murder, if it is the Enemy. The Terrorist can steal, cheat, rape, or torture; because it is the Enemy on whom he preys. All of the Enemy is guilty, regardless of individual responsibility. All of the Faithful are innocent, because they are faithful. This provides immunity for lack of morality, or desire for personal gain by criminal action. The only condition the Terrorist admits subjection to, becomes civilized behavior to the Faithful. The Taliban express how easy this admonishment is to evade, they have murdered thousands of their own people on the proclaimed charge of heresy; just anything, action or statement, which digresses from their own amendable policy.

The base practical position of Terrorism contains the implied statement human beings possess the right to kill other human beings and destroy human societies and their functioning, solely because such human beings and societies violate some ideal, ideology, or creed; which the Terrorist professes to hold dear. Humanity cowers condemned, because humanity will not submit to some ideological remonstrance; under the command of the Terrorists, as guardians of the Faith. The Terrorist exhibits increasing violence, the more sectarian and parochial be the Faith the Terrorist ascribes. The Terrorist presents the basic code of the Anarchist under the trappings of some ideal. Anarchy always asserted the tenant proposition anyone could be killed, for the crime of being different or disliked. The Terrorist feels compulsion only to define the dislike, to justify the sentence of Death.

4

Modern Humanism

The present World adheres to many philosophies, a general consensus among all but the radical; could be classified as Modern Humanism. The emphasis involves the burden of responsibility being placed on the Individual. It asserts the Individual should be the element held accountable for any action. This position may be as ludicrous as the position of the Terrorist; understanding the great restraints in modern society, for the Individual partaking of any independent action. No Individual can exercise any activity without at least the tacit support of a subsection of his Peers. The Terrorist, himself, must acquire funding, weaponry, and intelligence with which to plan Terrorist actions. It clarifies to the comprehension the Terrorist errors in blaming the entirety of society; but the magnitude of any action precludes any Individual from bearing sole responsibility for his activity.

The criminal culpability of Conspiracy must be altered for the fight against Terrorism. Human destruction will not stop, until all participants in Terrorism endure punishment for the furtherance of such criminality. Greater society will not allow full punishment of participants while the degree of guilt remains unrefined. The punishment must be exacted after this refinement, of significant magnitude to impel curtailment of Terrorist activity. The above statements beg an answer for definition of guilt and manner of punishment.

How can One define the degrees of guilt, when every Terrorist action be the result of a Group activity? The first step must contain the condemnation of the Group for eliciting such activity, which injured fellow humanity and greater society. Assignment of guilt to the Group responsible for said Terrorist action defined all in the Group to some degree responsible for the Terrorist action occurrence. Each must share some aspect of the punishment; determinant on their degree of participation in the decision-making function of the Group. The ideal punishment would be designed, so each participant finds punishment in the manner of his participation.

Religious leaders, ideologues, or Creed messiahs should be arrested, if they publicly advocate Terrorist violence; and sentenced to a period in Prison, where they are forbidden to practice their religion, ideology, or creed while in Prison. Religious artifacts, books on their faith, and contact with membership of their faith will be forbidden. Such Prisoners will be subjected to Press film of Terrorist actions during traditional periods of Prayer or meditation, as well as film bios of victims lost to such Terrorist attacks. The length of such sentences will sit with the Judges, and determined to last until a specific performance on the part of the Prisoner is attained. The Judges will assign a number of Books on the Rights of Man, and the position of Man in his society, for the Prisoner to read and internally integrate. The Prisoner will not be released until he has tested to a certain proficiency of understanding of said books; the number of books to be read determined by the Judges, to specify some minimum sentence. Prisoners will soon comprehend society will punish their participation in the advocacy of violence and Terrorism. Found knowledge of such Prisoners of the Terrorist attack before such attack took place, will incur the same punishment as the actual perpetrators at the assault.

Legislation in all Nations need be passed, stipulating the funding agents of all Groups engaging in Terrorist activities will be financially responsible for all losses incurred by such violence. Loss of life will have an average general 'wiegeld' assigned to each death and summed; all medical costs will be ascertained and summed; all physical plant destruction will be established and summed, plus the cost of all rescue and cleanup activities. The total costs will include the law enforcement costs of arresting the guilty and trial determination of guilt. The funding agents will be held responsible for all the above costs of a Terrorist incident. All funding agents' assets will be seized to pay for these costs, which will be paid to the same percentage per funding agent as financial assistance was provided to the Group, prior to the incident. A failure of sufficient funds held by the funding agents will entail a Prison sentence; of duration subtracting the daily labor value of all loss of life in the Terrorist incident per day, until such time as the total value of the cost of the incident is paid. Funding agents will learn funding radical groups, or fund-raising for them; becomes a very dangerous occupation.

Criminals which aids such Groups engaging in Terrorism must be assigned one-third of the guilt for such Terrorist attacks. The supply of false papers, money transfers, weaponry, or explosives will gain such Criminals one-third of the punishment. A terrorist attack which kills three or more Individuals leads to the Criminals answering charges of First Degree Murder. The Criminal must also face the individual sentencing of the set criminal sentences, for the criminal practices committed at the behest of the Terrorist group. Such Terrorist groups will soon be ostracized by normal Criminal elements, as too dangerous to work with.

Fellow membership of a Terrorist group, though not a direct participant in the Terrorist attack, must also be assigned one-third of the criminal responsibility of the terrorist attack. The participation in the creation of an environment calling for violence, easily equates to a one-third responsibility for the act of Terrorism. This simplifies the necessary conditions of Proof for law enforcement agencies. Two conditions alone must be proven by law enforcement agencies: proof that a specific Terrorist act was committed by a specific Terrorist group; and proof that the Individual belongs to the specific Terrorist group which committed the act in question. This practice will soon drain such organizations of new recruits.

'Carry-along baggage' concepts of assignment of guilt in criminal prosecutions may find much opposition from Courts dedicated to procedures originating in previous ages. Previous Terrorists and Mass Murderers used the Courts' insistence on peculiar minutiae has been witnessed; most notable where over half the Nazi leadership received only prison sentences with later release, even though the Group was responsible for the deaths directly of more than Six Million people, and indirectly responsible for the deaths of Sixty Million Europeans of all types during and because of World War II. The World today cannot withstand such evasion of personal responsibility; the potential for human destruction can be too easily constructed. Real, viable punishment which destroys the potential capacity for Murder must be implemented.

Many side issues need be considered in such an altered program. Innumerable members of such Groups guilty of Terrorist acts will claim they did not know the nature of such Groups, and therefore; they are free of guilt for such activities. The answer to such Individuals can only remain they helped create the environment where specific selection of members for inclusion in a inner-circle of murderers could take place. Innocent members of such Groups do not exist! Discussion of the destruction of other peoples or cultures holds the essence of guilt. The encouragement of radical, or more fanatical, elements of the Group; signs a desire to deny the rights of others. Professions of religious fervor hold no merit, if it results in the loss of human life. Membership in a Group stipulates a responsibility for the actions of that Group, even if membership is not a part of the leadership of the Group.

Many also will be the Criminals who protest they were lied to, in the purpose of purchase of their services by Terrorist groups. Simple reply states the involvement in criminal activity precludes a denial of personal responsibility. There was establishment of a criminal pattern, no matter what implied purpose asserted. The Criminal must learn his behavior will be punished by the legal forces of society; sometimes, the punishment will be excessive due to the final result of the injury to society. Lack of knowledge of the purpose of criminal activity must not absolve from the guilt of participation in that criminal activity.

Loud will become the cries of funding agents of such Terrorist groups; smitten by huge loss. Such funding agents will claim repeatedly they hoped only to fund Charities, Self-Help agencies, or organizations dedicated to the spread of their faith. Society must respond funding agents are guilty directly by the knowledge of what activities were being planned; or indirectly responsible by not insuring what purposes such funding would be put. The funding agents stay guilty, and assignable of punishment. Financial benefactors must learn to contribute only to respectable organizations, who publicly publish the manner of their expenditures. Such organizations will learn publication of their financial data can only increase contributions made; benefactors afraid to fund unknown organizations, and able to finance larger contributions to responsible organizations. Nations can aid in this effort by refusing tax deductions to Individuals contributing to organizations which do not publish their expenditure patterns.

The constraints placed on law enforcement agencies must also be reviewed, specifically in the acquisition of Intelligence on subversive groups. The most valuable Intelligence-gathering asset remains Wiretapping and electronic bugs. Most industrial nations possess wide restrictions on their use. The restrictions too severely hamper such a valuable asset. Civil liberties insist such use indiscriminately destroys the right against self-incrimination. The Author agrees; but proposes a different alignment for acquiring the necessary information, and protect against self-incrimination. This can be done by simple disallowance of any such information as evidence in any prosecution. Law enforcement agencies can learn what Individuals and subversive groups are up to; but have to base their arrests on evidence collected by alternate means. The law enforcement agencies will simply acquire the knowledge of where and when crimes have been committed, or when they will be committed. They will also acquire a data base on subversive groups and their membership. Enactment of law will allow for

Individual suit for damages incurred by financial loss or reputation, by unauthorized release of information on the Individual. The suits brought will be against the law enforcement agency responsible, with criminal penalties assigned to punish law enforcement officers who release information on Individuals without Court order.

National laws need to be enacted, where law enforcement agencies are allowed full access to Bank records, Corporate records, lists of Money transfers, and Charity records. The ability to file suit by Individuals against the law enforcement agency for release of information without Court order will be maintained; as well as criminal penalties for individual law enforcement agents. Law enforcement agencies will be allowed to order financial institutions of all types to tract the financial transfers of any Individual or Group, at any time. This acquired information can be used as Court evidence, because it is obtained from a Third-Party records audit. The Individual's use of the Third-Party organization signifies acceptance of external audit of such records.

The rules governing law enforcement agent use of force also served by reorientation. It will be transmuted in a Civil Suit procedure. Criminal penalties will be dropped in favor of indemnifications. Public Defenders will be allowed to initiate such Civil Suits against law enforcement officers. Payments for such found unjustified injuries will be made by garnishments of the law enforcement officer's wages, if found guilty of wrongful use of force. The Court will determine the extent of injury, the total costs involved by the injury, and the degree of guilt of the offending officer. The Court will then set of a garnishment level of such magnitude as to repay the injury, and properly punish the officer. Repeat offenders will be unlikely, because it directly affects the law enforcement officer's lifestyle. Instances of permanent injury will grant the Court option of dismissing the offending officer from law enforcement without pay or benefits. Murder will still be subject to criminal penalties. Law enforcement officers must testify against their fellow officers, or face dismissal from law enforcement service, without pay or benefits. Found perjury in such testimony will suffer the criminal penalties for such crime. The law enforcement agencies will enjoy no liability for abuse by offending officers; though the agency may have to pay a assignment to the Court for Contempt of Court, due to improper training procedures or incorrect hiring procedures. The Court, in addition, may assess a fine on the law enforcement agency for improper investigation of such incidents. All such fines assessed by the Court must be paid by the law enforcement agency as a garnishment on all officers' pay of Two percent of their wages per pay period, until the total assessment is paid.

Again there must come further change of modern social policy. Gone are the days where long intellectual debates can be entertained about criminal punishments, because of the intrinsic threat which criminal elements present today. Such physiological considerations of the mental state of the criminal at the time of the Crime, or his later potential conversion; cannot enter into the discussion of thwarting Crime. Capital Punishment (i.e., the Death Penalty) must be viewed as consent of the perpetrator to die as punishment, if he has ended another's life. Criminal defense claims of Insanity, Temporary Insanity, Lack of Prior Intent to Kill, Accidental Murder in the course of another Crime, and Murderous Negligence can no longer be heard. The worst defense this Author has ever heard of, is the case of a Triple Homicide whose defense was the Victims were standing behind law enforcement officers; who were firing upon him in the course of his escape from a bank robbery. The Criminal must grasp he will be killed by Society if he kills another human being; just as ruthlessly. The job of law enforcement devolves into simple proof the alleged Prep actually did the Crime; the Sentence becoming simple rote policy thereafter.

A fundamental alteration of Court procedure must come about; one which will be opposed by all lawyers, and most Judges. Legislation must be enacted, limiting the number of appeals after Conviction for a Crime to Three attempts at any level. These Appeals will be altered in nature as well; the Law will stipulate every Capital Crime trial must be reviewed by a Superior Court of Appeals. Their decision will be delivered as an Opinion, ordering retrial or Sentence concurrence. Defense lawyers will not be allowed to file Appeals based on any other possibility other than the innocence of their client. A final nail to impact into the limitation of the Criminal defense which must be found in enacted legislation; will be a limitation of defense fees paid to lawyers, a fine example could be limitation to the salaries drawn by the chief Prosecutor for the State; during the entire course of the Case. Popular Cause defendants must not be allowed succor, by an ability to raise huge legal war chests, or the wealthy granted immunity from punishment.

The Author realizes the great difficulty of implementing the above proposed Law; given the structural opposition of the entirety of the legal profession. It still motivates Society to limit the ability of purported officers of the Courts in their attempts to turn criminal prosecutions into a Cash-Cow for their own enrichment; a decided hindrance to the function of controlling criminality. The enforcement of such a Law would be easier than first appearance would exhibit. The chief Prosecutor for every Criminal Case could be charged with filing a form with IRS, stating the remuneration he received during the course of the Case. The IRS would insist the defense attorney file his actual fees from the Criminal Case. The IRS then would tax at rate of 100% any fees higher than the Prosecutors filed statement. Normal tax rates would apply to the rest of the defense lawyer's income. All officers of the Court, including defense lawyers, would quickly adopt procedures of efficient Court proceedings.

This Chapter's main concern has been with the needs of Society to alter it's procedures, in order to deal with the new added threat of Terrorism. The change from Individual Responsibility to Modified Group Responsibility makes a fundamental break with Western forms of Law, though it lessens in radical departure when compared with legal codes of the Mid-East and Asia. The use of unrestrained Group responsibility would indeed harm the rights of the Individual. Modified use of Group responsibility could place accountability more efficiently, than the current sole use of Individual responsibility. Western societies historically face great difficulty when confronted with Conspiracy, which does not conform to the normal patterns of Criminality; based as it is on ideology, rather than base personal desires. Only the assignment of the proper weight of guilt to each participant role of Terrorism can bring about the control and elimination of such aberrations.

The development of the structure of Law since the 1960s, both within the United States and the rest of the World, expresses serious deficiencies for the correct application of criminal penalties and Civil damage judgements. A primary detriment to the process lies in the adoption of Court procedures which require the freeing of Defendants, whose rights may have been violated. This insists on the dropping of charges against the Defendant, even if guilty of the charges, without any action taken against the offending law enforcement officer. The procedure does not protect the rights of the Crime victims, does not punish the Criminal, does not punish the violator of Civil liberties, and leads no one except the Crime victims into action to forestall future such activities. This Court procedure thereby punishes only the already suffering victims of predatory license. A sincere legal statement all must stand accountable for their own actions, whether they themselves have been victimized; must be introduced into the modern legal system. Secondary activity by others cannot negate original responsibility; but Secondary activity can increase legal sanctions, if the Secondary activity was generated by the original irresponsibility. This legal creed would hold each Individual accountable for the entirety of responsibility, which his conduct had caused.

The primary assertion of Society can only be a statement all are responsible for their own role in society. This role includes the impact of the Individual on others and their actions. The Author is reminded of the old definition of the limitation of free speech; 'One cannot yell Fire in a crowded Theater.' The actions of the mullahs in Pakistan comes to mind; starting riots because of a Government decision to aid the United States in the War on Terrorism. The determination must be reached as to where religious freedom descends into Insurrection.

The mullahs of Pakistan call for a Holy War against the United States, because of the American action against Afghanistan in the aftermath of the September 11, 2001 Terrorist attacks. The Government of Pakistan declared itself an ally of the United States in the endeavor.

The mullahs of Pakistan therefore commit treason in calling for a War against another nation, to which their own government wishes joint cooperation. The actions of the mullahs are not valid political dissent, and their encouragement of rioting is criminal insurrection. Many elements in this Country who opposed the Vietnam War would side with the position of the mullahs in Pakistan; and make the same mistake as made during their opposition in the Vietnam War. They prolong the Wars by a fragmentation of purposes; giving all participants false hopes as to final resolution; and forestalling effective diplomatic resolution of the Conflict. Almost all except the Author describe such activities as free speech and political action; it truly can be construed only as criminal incitement of crude ethnic passions.

Political action in any society entails the primary purpose of building consensus for a defined program of action. This consensus may be limited to a specific strata of society, and yet be political action. Political action ceases, and criminal malfeasance starts, when Civil strife is advocated. Law and Court must adopt a general rule for definition of the separation of Political Action and Criminal Unrest. The simplest expedient would assert any action to be Criminal, whose purpose is to disrupt the normal activities of the general populace in the area. Political Action is valid and remains so, if citizens can go about their daily affairs without major disruption. Destablization of citizens in the course of their daily necessities should initiate law enforcement action to limit criminal behavior.

The role of Journalism in the perpetuation of Criminal Unrest is legendary! The insinuation of sharp dissent has become the mainstay of modern Journalism. Photo-journalists do not turn on the cameras until the violence starts. Most such Events are staged, possibly not by the Journalists; but by the purveyors of unrest, activities do not start until the Cameras arrive. None risk the confrontation with law enforcement unless publicity for their minority opinions are assured. Journalists become equal Conspirators in the instigation of criminal activities, though like Monopolists of the current Age; constantly state no prior contractual agreements had been negotiated, they are simply notified where disturbances are to take place.

Freedom of the Press stands as a fundamental Western value, tied to the right of Freedom of Speech. Journalists, though, must be restrained from 'yelling Fire in a crowded Theater'. Laws need be enacted which define the limits to which Journalists can go. Photo-journalism could be restrained from showing any acts of violence in progress; allowed only to show damaged property, dead bodies, and Injured in the process of being treated. Criminal spokespersons who have led, sponsored, or been involved in criminal activities should be prohibited from being shown; though the statement of their desires or goals can be related by Journalists. Journalists can be mandated by Law to stipulate the official Government position on such activities, if they present the positions of such criminal spokespersons, in a concurrent time-frame of reportage. The final element of Law which could be introduced may be the licensing of Journalists without prejudice; requiring the passage of State or National Boards like many other professions, with loss of license for failure to maintain the standards dictated by Law.

Society must evolve to meet the imperatives of a more demanding Age. Qualification of old cherished beliefs and Rights can be conducted; without essential loss of the integrity of those values. The real necessity stays the maintenance of a free society; the destruction of which is the true desire of all Terrorists. Terrorism presupposes the destruction of liberty enjoyed by those independent of Terrorist megalomania. We, as a free people, must take action to protect Ourselves; without destroying Our own basic rights as a People. It stands as the Test which We must face and pass!

5

Validation of Fundamental Position

Western Civilizations tend to demand Society justify any subscription of the rights of the Individual. The Author, himself, ascribes to this tradition, feeling any subjection of the Individual to the greater Society; must come only from absolute apparent need to protect the rights of All concerned. Those We now face hold to a different acculturation, deeming an inherent right to demand a standard of behavior from all; according to some religion, creed, or ideology. Western thought perceives the Individual as entity with inalienable rights, only amendable in measures of protection; not in the effective provision of those rights to the Individual. Ideologues, whether religious, political, economic, or social in nature or combination, assert the Individual must be a subordinate element of a greater Whole. The Whole holding the sole rectitude of dispensation, according to it's own needs and desires; the Individual reduced to simple conformance to the demands of the Whole, which can punish the Individual for non-performance of demanded submission. Western culture holds Society remains nothing more than a composite of Individuals, who possess the right to be heard and pursue their own personal beliefs. Ideologues, who are most violently represented by Terrorism, believe the destruction of the Individual becomes intrinsic to the development of the Whole.

Part of the schizophrenia of Western society resides in the reality Religion has always been the development of an alternate Culture, with serious overtones of ideology. All religions define a specific personal code of behavior, to which all members must subscribe. Each religion claims there is a greater, higher Authority with the right to punish deviant membership. The principle of Individual condemnation exists in all religions, as it does in all ideologies. This proscribes the Individual will be punished for his failure to obey a higher, exterior, mandated code of behavior. This may or may not be the eventual fate for every Individual; the Author knowing nothing of the existence, or non-existence, of superior Authority. The trouble intrudes in the desire of Ideologues attempting to aid the defined Authority, in punishment of human failures to maintain the defined code of behavior.

Every religion on Earth has history of persecution of deviant minorities. Ideologues have always felt compelled to help their Deity punish the Infidel or Unfaithful, as outlined by themselves; with little assistance from their proposed God. Terrorism has always contained the worst aspect of the problem; but not the congestive power of the ideology. All membership suffers from the affliction; the best expression could be the provision of an example. Palestine turmoil has been with Us throughout Our lives. What is the basic problem between the peoples of the area? Almost all would claim the violence; but what is the violence based upon?

The basic Issue in the region still remains the problem of land division. Jews claim the region as their homeland and given to them by God; Arabs separated from legal land ownership, through lack of being Hebrew and following the edict of God. The Palestinians counterclaim the land in their birthplace, and Jews should not own the land because they are non-Muslim. Christians vow the land is the birthplace of their Lord and Savior, and should be open and free to all of their Faithful. Property rights of All have been corrupted by ideology. Jew cannot possess right to Arab land, for lack of submission to the Prophet. Arab cannot own Jewish land, because it is their homeland, given to them by God. Christian will not accept Arab or Jewish ownership of the shrines where Christ lived and walked; because they are not of the true Faith.

None will accept possession by the Infidel; the Muslim is not the sole culprit. Property ownership will never be legitimate in the area, because of ideology; any land dispersal detailing property of the Faith being held by Infidels. The perfect breeding ground for the violence-oriented ideologue, already specified at the Terrorist.

Investigation of Islamic anger against the United States is even more illustrative of the effect of ideology on all, not just the Terrorists. A common, repetitive charge made by Muslims against the United States comes from Our support of Israel. The fact surfaces that We actually support Israel only marginally. The United States provides as much military weaponry and assistance to Arab nations in the Mid-East, as We do to Israel. The United States provides more economic aid to Arab nations in the region, than to Israel. The United States conducts far more Trade with the Arab nations of the region, than with Israel. What is the criteria for Islamic anger of United States support of Israel? The resultant answer states the United States contains a significant Jewish minority of considerable wealth, who is resolute in their support of Israeli aspirations. This means Islamic anger at the United States derives from the fact many of Our more established Citizens happen to be Hebrew. This is the crime the United States committed against the Islamic world.

Moderate and Liberal Political sentiment in the United States suggest an alteration of U.S. Foreign Policy could pacify Islamic angers against the United States. The supposition must be considered prima facie false. Even moderate Islamic elements wants the entire region of the Mid-East under the control of Islamic Law. They would allow dissenters to reside in the region, but only with the rights and considerations allowed to non-believers in Islamic law. More Conservative Islamic elements desire old patterns of control of non-believers; such patterns best expressed by the Ottoman Empire, and Islamic control of Spain in the Middle Ages. The ideologues and radicals of Islamic thought show their preferences through the exhibition of the Taliban arresting a number of Americans for preaching Christianity. Ideologues in the Islamic faith would never surrender their anger at the United States; until Americans submitted to Islamic law (as defined by themselves). Aid packages and extension of Trade preference to Islamic nations will not deflect true Islamic aspiration. Americans must once again accept We do no possess the ability to entice foreign cultures to like Us.

The United States faces in the Islamic World an alien culture with an ideological base, founded on a religion previously bound to the conquest of non-believers. The Islamic faith has literally butchered hundreds of thousands, if not Millions, of human beings simply because they would not convert to the Islamic faith. The practice of Slavery continues to this day in many Islamic nations; though most Islamic nations possess laws against the institution, forced upon them by the Western Powers in the last Century. Almost every Islamic nation, even the most civilized like Egypt and Saudi Arabia, list several hundred deaths a year under the heading of Police Action. The rationale for these deaths, never defined for Western media, exists as the suppression of dissent. Islamic citizens do not possess the right of trial; the right of trial is granted only by Governmental authority, which does not mean Citizens are free from police harassment or punishment up to and including death. This is not the last danger to the Islamic citizen, who confronts the Warriors of Islam; a self-appointed band of radical Muslims dedicated to the purity of the Faith, expressed by the murder of radical mullah- condemned heretics. Islamic Governments rarely investigate or prosecute such executions. Americans have not endured such activities in Our society, since the U.S. Government forced the disbandment of the Avenging Angels of the Mormon faith.

The afore mention may seem like discrimination against the Islamic faith, but the Author would state it is the common philosophy of any Terrorist organization; and also the common Government policy of any Nation which sponsors Terrorism, regardless of particular ideology. The modus operandi of Terrorism must be examined. Inherent in every organization of Terrorism comes the commitment to the practice of murder. Every organization has some Judge or Committee of Judgement which adjudges individuals of such guilt, they can be killed. There exists no precise process by which an individual comes to the attention of this pseudo-Court; the individual will never hear a formal indictment against him. The Victim will also not be at the judgement hearing, or have defense counsel present during these proceedings. He is most often uninformed of the judgement against him, until he is kidnaped or killed. The manner of his execution is almost never stipulated, so the designated executioners can devise any torturous means they desire. A interesting notation of the procedure lies in the post-death condemnation of the Victims most often; to absolve an Executioner who acted in haste.

Islamic national leaders allow such executions to take place, for a number of reasons. The first and foremost being to escape condemnation by such tribunal. A primary reason for ignoring such atrocities comes out of desire to maintain public peace; all Terrorist organizations in Islamic nations have an uneducated class of Faithful, who are willing to riot upon the message of their leadership. Knowledge of Islamic social structure brings forth an additional reason for inaction; mullahs assert the sanctity of all forebears, no one is allowed to challenge the decisions or policy of previous Islamic leadership. A charge of blasphemy is laid against any challenger; with all mullahs joining in the accusation. The deprivations of previous Islamic leadership was so diverse and disjoint, any Terrorist action can be justified under their mantle. Terrorists need only to assert they acted as had a previous element of Islamic leadership, and all mullahs stay silent; no matter how horrid be the violation of human decency. Radical Islamic leadership confronts national leadership with charges they violate Islamic tradition, whenever national leadership attempts to control Terrorism. The distinction between traditional Islamic leadership exercising a unified power in the Islamic world, and fundamental criminals doing murder without mandate; never reaches public comment, because of fear of mullah condemnation. Islamic national leadership will never exercise effective control over Terrorists of the Islamic cults, until the power of all mullahs is broken. This will never happen unless national leadership introduces mass Public education for all citizenry, rather than religious schools controlled by the mullahs.

American foreign policy fares poorly in this matrix. Terrorist organizations preach hatred of the United States, and seek to commit atrocities against Americans. These Terrorist organizations are protected by radical mullahs, who claim religious tradition in this protection. All mullahs unite in defense of all claims of religious tradition, not matter how offensive Terrorist atrocities are to them individually. National leadership cannot condemn the Terrorist organization with appropriate action against them; without radical mullahs condemning the national leadership for their violation of Islamic tradition. The national leadership will not find any religious support at such condemnation; because of mullah union on issues of religious tradition. The national leader who would control Terrorism in his nation, will likely be a casualty of the Terrorism. American foreign policy demands active Terrorist suppression, and only alienates the national leadership involved.

United States Foreign Policy suffers one great detriment, this consisting of continuation of structural decisions which hurt American Interests among foreign populations from their inception. Initial alterations of American foreign policy are inevitably generated by American business interests, who are in pursuit of individual profits. The State Department attempts to justify what are often volatile demands made against aggrieved foreign peoples. These justifications establish a structural policy, where American prestige becomes an issue; perhaps the best explanation would be an effective example.

American Business Interests pressured the U.S. Government to recognize French claims to colonial possession of Indochina in 1945. They did so in exchange for French promises to grant American business special trading privileges in both France and Indochina. Reality stated at the time France would have had to grant such trading privileges in any case, due to the destruction of the French economy after

World War II. Roosevelt, and later Truman, bowed to American business demands; and allowed French reoccupation of Indochina. An insurrectionary movement almost immediately ensued; American business interests, at the behest of France, forced U.S. foreign policy to condemn this nationalist movement as Communist, and an assault upon Democracy.

France repaid American business interests by revoking the special trading privileges as soon as physically possible for France. France lost it's position in Indochina within eight years, leaving the region with puppet governments; which the United States was committed by foreign policy to sustain. All know the end result of the United States refusal to recognize legitimate political interests in the region. This would be an acceptable mistake, if it were the only mistake engendered in this manner.

American Oil interests pressured American foreign policy in the Middle East, ever since before the Second World War. The Oil interests provided this pressure for Arab assurances of cheaper and better oil production for the American Oil Companies. American foreign policy is currently singularly geared to placating Arab leadership. The end-result of over a half-century of this policy contains the fact there is not one Arab nation which can be considered a true democracy or Republic; based on the decision of the will of the people acting through effective political parties. No Arab nation as yet has universal Public Education; an absolute essential, if Arab nations expect to attain the productivity levels of a modern economy. Arab oil has risen from $4 a barrel, to over an average $23 per barrel for the last twenty years; Arab purchase less than half their imports from the United States, though over half of the American Trade deficit comes from funds shipped to the Arab nations for oil. The United States Munitions industry effectively armed everyone in the Middle East; making confrontation between Arab, Jew, Christian, and Terrorist ever more dangerous. The final comment states the United States has spent more for military deployments to the Middle East at the behest of Arab oil demands, than the United States spent on the entirety of the Vietnam conflict.

The United States must stop letting American business interests set American foreign policy, if America expects to garner good will among foreign peoples. Support or Condemnation of foreign regimes must be based upon the policies and behavior of those regimes; not the Profits picture of American trading partners of those Nations. A uniform statement of American foreign policy must be outlined, and then it's provisions followed. The United States must accept dealing with all legitimate political interests, not just those who make promises or commitments to American business interests. The policy of American military intrusion on the behalf of foreign interests must be stopped. Such military excursions, when conducted, must be to fulfil American national interests, be of overwhelming force, and completely effective in design and scope. They must end on a timetable established by American leadership, whether all objectives are completed or not. All foreign nations, and Terrorists, shall learn American response is rapid, relatively effective, and of high impact; though of limited duration. This regenerates the Teddy Roosevelt policy of 'Walk softly, but carry a big stick.'

The final point of this Chapter compels the expansion of action against Terrorism beyond security measure and military action. All Terrorist organizations utilize propaganda for purposes of recruitment, and gaining support inside native populations wherein they base their operations. Western intellectualism must confront this propaganda, and defeat it. American Educators, religious leaders, Political Scientists, and Economists must be enrolled along with qualified native language translators for the exact purpose of destroying the message of Terrorism. They must analyze all documentation on which Terrorists base their ideology, provide effective Western intellectual thought to condemn the usage of such documentation for impelling violence along with finding condemnation in native thought, and translate this response into the native languages of the peoples subjected to Terrorist propaganda. The United States Government, along with other Western nations, must insure this response reaches the native peoples; possibly through broadcasts like America Free Afghanistan, but more beneficially through purchase of air-time of native TV and radio, newspapers and magazines, and publishable library sources.

A number of stipulations need be made concerning the above program of action. Effective academic refutation of Terrorist claims must be unchallengeable, both in Western thought and in native thought. Native language translation must be flawless, without hidden gaffs. The use of natives themselves, or First-generation emigrants, guarantee the only surety of the accuracy of translation. Native religious leadership of moderate inclination will bring authenticity to the Project; but their overt involvement along with the involvement of the translators will have to be hidden, for the safety of the Individuals. The quality of the scholarship must be unassailable, and the means of it's decimation must be trustworthy to the native population. Western thought must have clear exposition to native populations; and native intellectual thought must be shown to actually counter Terrorist claims. The end-result must be an expansion of native intellectual thought, without assertion of Western national policy aspirations for the area. The effort must be free of taint, and cognizant of native national desires.

6

Human Codes of Conduct

What contains the exact function of the Individual within his society? Many supply both full and partial answers; often without awareness of the ramifications of their replies. Nietzsche claimed the Individual was at the service of the State; the sole rightful guardian of the destiny of the Individual, who was simply food and limb for the greater organism. Ideologues practice the same diminishment of the Individual to Group will, though they have abandoned the State for whatever cherished Ideal they would stipulate. Thomas Paine and Thomas Jefferson claimed inalienable rights for the Individual, though each asserted the Individual was compelled to fight for Liberty. Anarchism claimed Individual Will was sacrosanct, and the right to destroy other Individual Will by violence. Ideologues refined the words of Nietzsche, evolving the context of Totalitarianism. Western thought developed the concepts of Paine and Jefferson to establish both concepts: Democracy and Republic. Terrorism adopts the format of both Anarchism and Totalitarianism to formulate Civil insurrection.

Terrorism proclaims there exists an absolute totalitarian Ideal to which all must submit; whether it be their wish and belief, or their deepest aversion. Individual choice evaporates in the context of the absolute nature of the Ideal. The Individual must submit, or be destroyed. True Believers escape any punishment for any human misconduct, if committed for furtherance of the Ideal. The Individual finds salvation by acting in concert with the Ideal, no matter what his personal transgressions; the Individual stands condemned, if he violates the covenant of the Ideal, or does not believe in the Ideal. Terrorism completes the cycle, by assuming the rectitude of action, in being the defender of the Ideal. Terrorists can remind of the criminal 'Son of Sam' who claimed to kill, because a dog told him to do it. Terrorism claim the voice of the Ideal instructs; who or whatever such a Voice is.

Islam sits as the religion most susceptible to the trappings of Terrorism. The Prophet, himself, maintained he received the message of Allyah while fasting in a cave in the mountains. One does not need to contest the factuality of the Account; simply to relate a Deity seemed strapped for resources, if such is required to talk to his chief Prophet. Physical stresses of hunger and cold most often bring hallucination, rather than illumination. Irrespective of which was derived in the Cave; One can wonder at the viability of a Code of Salvation derived in such manner, without countervailing commentary. The Author wishes to apologize to his Islamic brethren; simply stating his lack of understanding of the process of miracles. He would also state American Indians use such physical stresses to gain revelation. The process still retains a troubling aspect; especially when connected to a Code of Behavior to which all are to submit. Such revelations, derived in like manner, repeat throughout the history of Islam.

Teachings of Christianity also present troubling aspects as well. A fundamental tenant of Christianity states Christ died to absolve others of their sins. One asks whether it would not have been better to punish people for their sins, so people would not commit such transgressions once more. An omnipotent, all-seeing God is to be the Judge at the end of days; to determine if One receives Heaven or Hell. The all-seeing Deity should have made the Judgement earlier, to save an incredible degree of strife. The apparent blasphemy is advanced for specific purpose; not an attempt on the part of the Author to ridicule those of the Faith. The Presentation forwarded indicates a sound principle in examination of human conduct; religion itself stands as a poor vehicle to assess personal responsibility in action. Religion follows the laws of God; We have need to devise the laws of Man.

The laws of Man cannot be an imitation of the laws of God, because We are trying to save Man from Man; not to save Man for eventual Salvation. The laws of Man must consider the order of Society, and the protection of the Individual; at least until such time as the Individual is called to God. The Confessional serves the purpose of God; Man needs to impose greater punishment than Prayer. The Deity of the Author would agree Forgiveness serves the realm of the Hereafter, not the Courts of Man. The Reciprocal of the thesis states acting in the Deity's name cannot be a defense in the Courts of Man. Crime against Man still retains the essence of Crime against Man, and must be answered in a Court of Man. Religious or other ideological claim does not absolve from responsibility to the laws of Man.

Many wonder how what they consider the finest part of Mankind, his religious belief; could be used as vehicle to support Terrorism. The answer must come from a study of the development of all Religions on the Earth. Religion as Faith and as complex of beliefs originated in much earlier periods of human history. Each religion promises a better life or Greater state, if the faithful abide by the rules of the religion. Now many cultures of the World find themselves with little hope of advancement; also faced with the lifestyle and development of the Western industrialized Nations. It was no mistake when Taliban leadership declared the American people must be destroyed, and thrown out of Heaven. American society represents to these backward cultures a better life, which they cannot hope to attain in this lifetime. Religions of these retardant cultures witness Americans; believing Americans to be living the effective afterlife, which they had been promised by their religion. The major problem of all religions on the Earth resides in the reality, such religions do not provide for technological expertise. Mullah, Priest, Rabbi, Buddhist monk, and Minister should all unite in calling for Education in practical skills, not destructive behavior.

Claim of Revolutionary zeal compared to the physical acts of Terrorism; classify Terrorism as non-revolutionary. Terrorists do not attack despotic regimes, opting destructive violence only for open societies where they can operate freely. Terrorism presents no revolutionary program of action; simply calling condemnation on an entire people, who will not abide by a code of behavior set by the Terrorist. The attacks contain no implied intent to destroy the structural forces of Government in the assaulted area. No attempt to bring down the Government, and supplant it; exists in either Terrorist ideology or practice. The Crimes a Terrorist purports a society commits and therefore, need be destroyed; are not coherently stated, or even rationally outlined. Terrorism distills only to simple envy of the success of others; with the desire to destroy such success. Terrorism rests on the most nihilistic of base emotional emotions; the desire to reduce all to their own level, as the Terrorist can rise.

Two fundamental positions have always existed in human society; one is the principle the Individual should work and earn that which he has, the other insists on the right to steal what others earned for their own enrichment. Society always stood upon the principle of the Working Individual and property rights. The human race confronts a much different scenario Today. There exists great disparities of lifestyle and standards of living between co-existent cultures. This disparity came about by the underlying position of each culture to the principle of universal education. The successful societies of the Present started practices leading to universal education more than a Century ago. The societies failing in the current economy and World structure, are exactly those who have started universal education only some decades back; or have yet to adopt such educational practices. The populations of failing cultures blame successful cultures for their problems, when it is truly failures of their own societies which led to their malaise. Failing societies and their people turn to criminal philosophy of theft, rather than adopt the hard effort to educate their people.

The matrix of human social context distorts in most regrettable challenges to what was previously considered proper social concourse. The expansion of the human population exacerbates the dip to criminal behavior. This affects even successful cultures by glorification of the activities of the socially deviant. The acquisition of Wealth becomes the superceding goal, all sacrificed to that end. Right and Wrong reduce to methodologies for attaining success, defined as further aggregation of Wealth. White Collar criminals steal more than any bank robber ever could acquire Capital in liquid form, and get off with community service and token fines; through the purchase of huge legal services for hire. Neighborhood heros become local drug pushers, who wear and show the trappings of Wealth. The new Upper Class consist of Corporate raiders, noted for defrauding Employees of long-established retirement plans and medical care. Indicative of the alteration in social priorities is the practice of Fund Raising, where over half of the raised funds of traditional Charities go to payment of professional fund-raisers; a class of Individuals who maintain six-figure incomes by extolling the plight of the Poor.

Failing human cultures exhibit even greater horrors to social functioning. The Heros of the people become those who attack the vestiges of Wealth. A profile Americans can understand would be the criminal culture of the Great Depression, or post-Civil War South. Jesse James, John Dillinger, Bonnie and Clyde, Ma Barker, and Baby-faced Nelson all became heros because of their attacks upon Banks and Railroads. Failing cultures Today produce suicide bombers, who are raised to the rank of cultural heros. Their sole effort to attain this rank was the destruction of some symbol of entrenched Wealth; be it the World Trade Center, or only a bus in downtown Tel Aviv. The role is exactly the same as the gangster of the Thirties; destroyers of the symbols of Wealth and Stature. The generative drive of such action comes from Envy; a hatred of the opportunity of others for a lifestyle superior to their own.

The concentration on the above data comes from a realization no impetus to end the violence will derive, until the inequality between cultures is eliminated. Such an equality could never exist, without an equality of Education. The possibility of a spread of Education of this magnitude stands as nil; for the current existing populations of failing cultures, absolute zero. Less than one percent of all adults over Twenty years of age can be expected to gain two more years of education; if starting from the position of illiteracy, only one in 23,000 adults can expect to learn to read. Only One out of 70,000 of the above can be expected to have read more than ten books, after whatever primary education they did attain. An improvement in these failing cultures will come only with the universality of primary education; an effectual possibility only for future generations. The ability to read and perform basic mathematical calculations must be the threshold attained, so modern economic performance becomes capable.

Reversion to the purpose of the Chapter calls for evaluation of the material presented. The concept Terrorists have justification for their actions because of some religious or ideological affiliation, must be absolutely and firmly refuted. The assertion Terrorists are only working for a better World must also be rejected; it has been shown Terrorists possess no revolutionary program, no effective program for replacing the current Governments, and no alterations of social conduct which is conjoint, rational, or debatable. The breeding ground for Terrorism suffers from it's own deficiencies, for which more advanced societies can present only limited assistance. The reality asserts advanced societies possess only the ability to survive the populations of the failing societies, and no ability to save those populations. Advanced societies should apply all pressure possible, insuring primary universal education is extended in these failing societies to all of the Young. This will allow for failing societies to evolve into participating elements of the World economy. Once the threshold of primary education is reached by all in failing cultures, integration with the advanced societies becomes possible.

The development of the modern economy bred much of the impetus of Terrorism. Modern technology brought an unheard spread of Communication; traditional societies tied in a developmental stasis for centuries were confronted with vastly superior modes of lifestyle. Traditional visions of Heaven were challenged by visual presentations of

Lifestyle, reminiscent of the Garden of Eden to the uneducated populations of the stasis cultures. More advanced medical practices achieved in successful cultures insisted on spread into failing cultures; with resultant increase of population levels, which instituted social stress upon traditional production practices. Failing cultures had to accept Trade products from the advanced cultures, else disintegrate from the population pressures. These Trade products began to replace traditional products through their greater efficiency; destroyed the viability of traditional occupations. Failing cultures found themselves with increasing population, and shrinking opportunities for labor employment. The populations of these failing cultures began vocalizing sentiments shown by Black intercity populations in the 1960s; the difference only it was not resentment against their own upper class, but anger at the more advanced societies. The marketing practices of business of more successful cultures continue to express the inferiority of these failing culture populations, in hopes of increased Sales of product. Uneducated peoples cannot escape the continuous bombardment of verbal and visual identification of their own inferior lifestyle; and lack of opportunity surrounds them, informing they will never achieve the success of the advanced societies.

This information insists much of the antagonism towards successful societies by failing cultures could be eradicated by a limitation of Marketing efforts to those areas, where no possibility of purchase exists for the majority of citizenry. Laws should be enacted in more successful societies constraining marketing efforts for any product, or product line; to the areas where such products would provide economic advantage. This could be stated simply as a Law stipulating a product must meet Government established criteria for sale in the area. Successful societies' Governments could work with the Governments of failing societies to stop counterproductive sales and marketing. These Governments could also work together to forestall much of the offensive transference which aggravates the population; the sole agreement the Author has with the Taliban regime in Afghanistan, was the arrest of

Christian missionaries in the country. Those missionaries were not in Afghanistan in a serious effort to convert, simply to confront an Islamic regime. Other efforts Governments could impede is the spread of literature, movies, and TV programing which is culturally offensive; one serious way would be the limiting of sale of TVs and radios able to receive foreign broadcasts. This would require a distribution of band widths for regional use. Another avenue would be a Universal Law of Internet use, where Webmasters would have to block regional assess, or have fines imposed by foreign governments collected by their own government. The entire result would be a lessening of friction between societies.

A further initiative of great value could be explored, though it would probably face great opposition. This would an International Treaty establishing an International Textbook Commission; an organization composed of multi-national membership. The Commission would be detailed to orchestrate guidelines for acceptable textbooks, free of cultural bias and egocentric exposition of history. The Commission would be authorized to select the acceptable textbooks used in all primary and secondary educational systems; with each member-nation able to blackball five textbooks per grade level per year. The Commission would also be entailed with ensuring all texts were translated effectively into each language necessary. There would be legal stipulation that at least five textbooks be available for use in every Grade level and subject; so actual educational systems would have a selection choice. Most of the World could not understand the importance of such an effort, so the Author will attempt an explanation.

A great Wit once stated the United States and Great Britain were separated by a common language. This commentary expresses the importance understanding of basic concepts, with common definitions for the words used. The unification of textbook structure would do more for the understanding between peoples, than could even the adoption of one universal language. The manner Each in a debate approaches a problem alters the understanding of the problem, and the grasp of the potential solutions. An International Textbook Commission would be desirous of a common structural presentation, than any consideration of content or application of particular histography. Some Educators would argue this formulation detracts from scientific exploration; yet the benefits vastly outweigh any shortcomings. The World can learn to understand other things, after people have come to understand one another.

Politicians and national educators spent incredible amounts of intellectual verbiage on the concept of One World; hubris claiming societies are growing more interrelated, due to the advances in Communications and Production. The reality insists societies polarize more with the advent of successive links of communication; cultures impacted more seriously with potential counter-culture values. One of the most controversial elements of cross-cultural pollination lies in the desire of Islamic women to dress with Western modes of dress. The Author totally empathizes with the women on the issue; but nevertheless, traditional values are violated. The Buddhist women of South East Asia are to be found in jeans and T-shirts more often than sarongs; simple awareness to signify it is not only the machismo of Arab men which finds offense. Japanese traditionalists bemoan the fact western-style bathrooms with showers replace the bathhouse culture of old. London East-enders and Dublin workers curse the big-screen TVs blaring sporting events in their Pubs. The Author complains he cannot get a Ham-Salad sandwich and bowl of vegetable soup in any restaurant in his hometown; he dislikes Greek and Sushi. All cultures suffer from heightened competition over cherished values, with independence of choice a seeming degradation of traditional cultural values.

This clash of cultures becomes battle between marketing agencies to sell greater amounts of their products in the designated markets, than competing companies touting products of another sectional culture. Little marketing efforts are designed to promote traditional products and services; only in the generation of new tastes in the consuming market. Traditionalists watch the airways, believing their culture has been dismissed; as old-fashioned and obsolete. Consider the last time one has heard 'Drive the U.S.A. in your Chevrolet'. You will find it difficult to hear or see 'Chevrolet' or 'Chevy' at any General Motors dealership; marketing strategies insist new and compelling terms must be constantly used. Members in their culture lose the common thoughts and precepts of their Youth; and blame foreign cultures for the loss. Broadcasts treats items of Youth as if they were a dusty collage found on the back shelf of a library; quaint oddities once conducted by an extinct species of dinosaurs. The practice intensifies the feeling traditionalists endure of separation from their origins.

Government, Educator, and Broadcaster need combine for a presentation of continuity in society. The passage of Time turned to a evolution and growth of society, not a radical truncation of previous society roots and limbs. Abandonment of old ways shown as advancement of old values, not tossed garbage to buy new. The resentments of Age must be reduced, by clear presentation of their role and place. The angers of Youth turned from the paths of revolution, into communicating with Elders of the potentialities of change. The principle of Inclusion must include respect for all generations; with recognition all Ages deserve acceptance of their goals. Equal voice will bring equal Peace; something produced by little else.

7

Role of Man

Philosophers attempt continually to define the Role of Man; a subject debated since the dawn of society. Almost all religions find origin in some definition of the Role of Man, each describing a slightly altered version based upon the concept of a Supreme Deity. Older religions outline a pantheon of Gods, where warfare betwixt the deities determined the fate of Man. The newer religions suggest a major Deity, with lesser malignant immortal beings trying to destroy Mankind; at least some version of destruction as called forth by religious leadership. All religions claim some mode of behavior be mandatory, for the escape from destruction. It remains sufficient to recount each mode of behavior serves the religious leadership, in attainment of very secular goals on Earth.

The mullahs in Afghanistan and Pakistan call for a religious war against the United States; not precisely to fulfil the will of Allyah, but to serve very political purposes here on Earth. It once served Vatican purposes not to receive reports from Polish bishoprics during World War II; substance detailing the Nazi Extermination camps on Polish territory. The Patriarch of Moscow felt it prudent not to comment on Serbian 'ethnic cleansing' practices in the Balkans. The Southern Christian Conference condemns homosexual marriage and Sex Education in schools; but has not yet issued a condemnation of illegalities committed against the Blacks in the South, during the era of the Ku Klux Klan. These are commentary on positions held by prior religious leadership, which many would find offensive; mentioned here only to state religious policy often follows the lines of secular politics. The

Author will assure he does not belief any Deities of any Faith would deviate in their message.

The complexities of positioning of Religions and their leadership impels the Author in doubts, as to the abilities of religion in defining the Role of Man. The concept of a Deity, itself, finds little root with the Author; unless the Deity enjoys a root connection with humanity. He settles for the belief the Supreme Deity exists only as the subconscious mind of the entirety of the human race. Such definition leads to a nullification of the principle of infallibility, as well as the principle of omnipotence. The Deity could only be as effective, as the humanity which spawns the Being. Clear evidence easily found can express an evolution of Deities; else a greater human awareness of Supreme desire. Deities worshiped Today once condoned slavery, the subjugation of women, and the torture and killing of heretics. Gods seem to get more human, as Civilization advances. Many secular Intellectuals feel the need to extrapolate the words of the Deities for their fellow men. The Author moves forward, confident he furthers the work of the Lord; possibly the will of other Supreme Beings.

Mankind's essential need stands as establishment of a matrix for human activity, i.e., society. This matrix calls for certain guarantees granting human habitation the ability to prosper. The primary need for self-protection, protection of personal property, secure and safe employment, and provision of the basic human needs of food, shelter, and companionship. It is distinctly noticeable these are the precise areas which Terrorists and Totalitarian regimes attempt to destroy. Humans cut from this matrix of safety, find themselves defenseless; no ability to labor for the benefit of human life allowed. Terrorist and Totalitarian pervert the normal matrix, unsuccessfully attempting to supplant normal human behavior; with an agenda of their own device, hoping to create a submissive slave system.

Clarity of exposition demands evaluation of the intrinsic errors of slave systems. Economies serve as distribution of products for satisfaction of human needs. They, as un-managed systems, delegate supply of products according to the amount of labor performed by each element in the system. This distribution of products provides incentive to each laborer to perform industriously, seeking to fulfil his own personal desires and the desires of his dependents. The beauty of the un-managed system comes from the manner productive decisions derive. Previous successful labor determines what level, and direction of production will be conducted in the future; resources flow naturally to those sectors most desired. Labor elements decide what degree of taxation and devotion of resource should be detailed for infrastructure and national defense. Successful labor elements express expertise in systems' development; best capable of understanding the demands of public need. Slave systems seek to distort this pattern of development, to alter production direction and distribution processes.

The primary goal of any slave system desires emplacement of an aristocracy, based on criteria other than economic performance. Elements of the aristocracy wish the luxuries of the most successful labor elements in the economy, but possess none of the economic skills. They could never attain their desire under a normal economic process. Their covetousness leads to the proposition of violating the civil liberties and property rights of economic labor elements, through the use of force and terror. They began their campaign to subjugate labor elements by the killing or torturing of dissidents, who would demand their fair share of the economic wealth. This initially destroys the most productive economic elements, with correspondent decline in economic performance. The aristocracy then begins to demand the luxurious products of the previous successful labor elements. The Economy has already endured decline because of the loss of the most productive elements; the demands of the aristocracy place huge additional burden on the remaining economic labor elements, suffering from skilled labor shortages. The Economy must devote an excess percentage of resource to production of luxury products for the aristocracy; again, with a serious loss of economic performance. Less successful labor elements find their labors can no longer supply the basic necessities they need, to maintain their own economic performance. The increased resistence to the exorbitant demands of the aristocracy incites the aristocracy to perform more horrendous atrocities, to cow the populace. These practices mean even greater economic labor assets lost, and reduced production. This stands as the basic degeneration of economic function, and occurs in every form of slave system devised; even types of hidden systems.

Examples of hidden slave systems can be found even in the American economy. The Author has intimate knowledge of current strategies limiting the income levels of published authors, for the enrichment of publishing companies. This constriction of Author income reduces the quality of literature, curtails the availability of diverse storylines, and forces Authors to concentrate solely on money-making efforts with loss of Individual development and expression. The reading Public gains nothing in reduction of book cost, on the contrary; publishers begin to raise the costs to readers, in maintenance of the luxurious Profits. The debacle of the publishing industry, though, reminds only of the greater malaise in American society; the huge concentration on Corporate profits, at cost to product quality, and labor protection. Costs to Consumers rise, as quality falls; Consumers joining the ranks of employees, injured by embedded resistance to fair dispersal of the advantages of production.

All slave systems, whether overt or covert, degenerate the economic process. Successful labor elements lose the resources to develop fully, while the distortion in dispersal of product leads to concentration on production for the aristocratic classes; who lack the expertise to normally derive such profits and products. Slave systems devolve into only special forms of parasitism, destroying natural development of economic leadership, and reducing productivity by concentration on production of product satisfying the desires of the created aristocracy. Few authors examine the curtailment of the Middle Class in America, victims of parasitic Corporate profits-taking. The Taliban in Afghanistan reduced economic productivity in the Country by Sixty percent, prior to the American bombing. Afghani citizens found their diet cut to a quarter of it's previous sustenance, while Taliban elements ate heartily. Slave systems distort the economic process, with accelerating degeneration over time.

Return to the original argument of this Chapter decrees the Role of Man outline, create, and maintain a matrix under which a society can be formed. Sufficiency of matrix demands protection from the natural elements and disasters, protection from natural and human predators, establishment of a functioning economy, and methodology for the resolution of issues affecting the matrix, the society, or both. The final goal and result hopes for the development of Civilization; a structure where children can be raised and educated, the level of physical and economic distress reduced to acceptable levels, and every element of society can labor for their own betterment.

The degree of Communal interaction necessary calls for a Governmental structure to assure minimum standards of living are attainable by every element, development of an educational structure so future elements of the labor force acquire the basic skills mandated, and criminal action cannot destroy the gains made by the labor elements in their employ. The above details an intensity of governmental specialization. A special self-defense force organized for controlling criminal behavior, combating natural disasters like fire and flood, and maintaining rescue operations for cases of accident and illness. This force may be constructed by integral elements of the Work force if the Community is sufficiently small; but must be an institutionalized discrete force, as the level of burden rises. The composition does not matter, except some form of taxation must exist to pay for the expenses of this self-defense force.

The function of the Education of future elements of the labor force requires the raising of a distinct labor specialization, unless a system of Apprenticeship evolves. Such a system produces very effective labor elements, but lacks in specific areas; the Master must have sufficient wealth he may devote a significant amount of his time to training apprentices, the number to be educated does not exceed the capacities of the Master to teach, and there are sufficient placements in the economy for the new apprentices to occupy. Apprenticeship becomes quickly overburdened with increase in population, and rises in productivity which reduce placement positions. Specialized labor for Education purposes must take over when apprenticeship fails. This specialized labor requires establishment of occupational standards, as provision of a salable product in the economy. Society, through Government, often discovers it must assume the payment for Educational labor; private elements prove to insufficiently fund the training, adversely impacting the relevant skills of future labor elements. Another Communal taxation must be imposed.

Politics and Law enter the Forum as issues have need of resolution, and minimal observance of the rights of each member of the society must be considered. Delegated Individuals must be chosen to decide issues, and to assess the guilt of violators of the rights of members of society. These chosen can be integral members of society, if the community remains small enough, such work can be conducted outside of normal economic endeavors of the chosen Individuals. Sufficient magnitude of Population insists these functions evolve into occupational positions, made by some form of Communal taxation.

Relief from economic failure brings the requirement of private charity, until and unless the levels of economic failure become too great; when such relief can only be conducted by Government welfare measures. It is at this time Government subsidy becomes another form of Communal taxation. The rationale for Government subsidy resides in recuperation of economic failure for future economic performance, proper nourishment for future economic labor elements, and reduction in physical stress of economic privation. The causal order of subsidy to avoid economic distress lies in the more harmonious future functioning of the economy, as well as maintaining realistic consumption of current production.

The above discussion expresses the functionality of obligation a labor element enjoys, over and above his personal contribution of effort; this can be categorically termed Communal taxation. It in generalized form dictates the level of effort each labor element owes to Community service. The monetary nature of most Communal taxation simply signifies Community awareness of the advantages of specialization of labor; with each labor element working at his selective choice, and employing specialized labor for such service. The intricate argument simply asserts each labor element has obligation to pay for the benefits of Community, a debt paid through taxation. Tax-evaders deny their obligation to the Community. Modern Republican Party thought mocks the generative needs of the Community, by insistence the needs of the Community be borne by those most often in need of such services. The Wealthy derive their Wealth from the Economy and Society; their debt, if anything, remains greater, as assets are substantially more.

The Individual must be willing to engage in defense of the Community, especially for the weaker and less fortunate. Rationale states the unproductive elements of society increase in number without communal action, loss of future labor and consumption reducing the attainment of all in society. It works equally in the political sphere, rights denied to a segment of society will be extended to more elements of society; as the leadership of society discerned benefit from such limitations. Either of the above issues will initiate some form of slave system, which will bring down the standard of living of all. The Individual owes his labor, communal taxation, and defense of those who cannot defend themselves.

The final thrust of the Chapter turns to the entire spectrum of individual liberties. Many define civil liberties as those individual demands, which a proponent demands for himself. The upshot conclusion being One cannot take from others, that which is insisted for Oneself. This decision lacks precision, and suffers from fanciful escape from the impact of economic production on different elements in society. There is the concept of freedom from physical assault; yet Citizens uniformly require Police and Military to risk just such physical assault without thought. There is the concept of the right to work for the betterment of Self; most who make this claim belong to the more profitable labor elements, and refuse to accept a concept of a living wage for all. There is the concept of Property with residual rights; most proponents adamantly denying Profit-sharing with employees. All of the above illustrate a 'pick and choose' mentality concerning the rights to be upheld or rejected.

The best approach to individual liberties may be the concept of minimal standard of life for all. This carries serious hazards as well; a innate justification to steal or assault, if the standard of living of an Individual did not reach a specific level. This is a position which no society could sustain. Sharp examination finds this avenue enduring many other defects, the most major consisting of the laziness and ineptitude of certain elements of society. Also embedded within this approach lies the resistence of elements to training, or re-training, for productive labor. It finally ignores the above-average efforts of labor elements seeking a better life.

A splayed pattern to the enforcement of individual rights leads to enforcement of some, while ignoring the hard to enforce elements. All societies today pretend to dispense Justice equally in their laws and Courts. The reality remains of poorer elements of society being universally victimized by law enforcement action, while the wealthier elements of society habitually receive minimum sentencing; even when poorer elements could prove their innocence with proper representation, and where wealthier elements often steal much greater amounts of economic capital. Workers, Police, and Military traditionally receive far less for physical injury and stress endured under demand of their employers, than the remuneration levels demanded by those same employers. Skill levels of employees are underpaid, simply because they are employees; whose employers insist on total ownership of patent rights and production. Corporations insist on the same legal rights as an individual Citizen, but refuse to accept the same liabilities as a Citizen; concerning physical assaults upon Individuals, i.e., Corporations can poison Individuals without criminal sanction. A uniform code of Individual Rights need to be devised and enforced.

This Author has determined society should adopt the approach of demanding a certain level of performance from every Individual. This attitude would require vast increase in Government involvement in individual lives, thought repugnant to the Author; yet still containing the essentials for communal success. The essence of this concept lies in the demand of society that each Individual list a gainful employment of some minimum hours per week; else they be forced to report for communal employment, if they are to receive any Government subsidy of any type. Wealthier elements of society living on the profits of earlier employment of themselves or their forebears must do the same; if they do not have gainful employment, they must report for communal employment or pay a special tax equal to the gainful communal employment of the Individual for a year. This measure would have nothing to do with normal tax rates, and would help immeasurably in control of Criminal elements.

Opponents of the above scheme will insist such would be a vast increase in the cost of Government. It not be the case! Unemployed could be ordered to attend classes (or teach them), qualifying them for more gainful employment. They could be instructed to clean up their own neighborhoods; a portion of the property tax could be devoted to renovation of property, to pay for street-cleaning, garbage and Junk pickup, and painting. Many could be utilized in Child-care supervision, handling neighborhood children while the Parents worked. They could be employed in construction or renovation of Government buildings, Parks, and recreational facilities. An important element of the Unemployed could engage in Restoration and Preservation efforts; ranging from restoration of old buildings to transcribing old library texts to electronics for Print on Demand reproductions. Sufficient outlets for employment could be found or devised.

The principal accomplishment of such a Program would be elimination of the disincentives to employment; everyone would be required to labor, so the worst aspect of Welfare is eliminated. Those most unfortunately inept in economic function could be retrained. Business could be enrolled in the effort, under Government-funded apprenticeships; costing no more than Welfare payments do today. Medical costs overall could be reduced, by Government sponsorship of elimination of health hazards. Economically depressed areas can gain economic stimulus, by a heightened level of economic activity. A sense of Community and self-accomplishment can be generated in previously unemployable. The Individual, in the final analysis, would be induced to seek better employment; laboring for the Government essentially 'shit details', and low-paying.

There will be great objection to this Program, with claims it violates the rights of the Individual. These can be easily countered, by statement a society has obligation to provide an environment where an Individual can fulfil his economic needs; without extending the advantage of Parasitism. Others will allege it will overburden the Government with expenditures; the unwillingness of wealthy elements to show up for communal service, will generate a large Fund for the Program. This could be vastly extended by insistence all Social Security beneficiaries endure the same sanction, if their said benefits constitute less than twenty percent of their total income; such charge not to be greater than the level of their income benefit from Social Security. Corporations which pollute can be made to pay fines, which are a percentage of Management salaries and benefits along with Stockholder dividends in the offending years; fines assessed as 10, 20, 50, or 100% of said funds in additional tax. Business can be allowed less than industry cost for labor, say Two or Three Dollars an hour paid to Government; if they establish qualifying apprenticeship programs for Communal service workers. Educational institutions must accept Communal service retrainee students, in order to receive Government funding; at rates not greater than 75% of the tuition costs of normal students. The costs to Government of this Program could be lower than the current costs, with vast increase in economic activity.

The Individual has been found as responsible, as well as endowed, by his position in society. He possesses right to the advantages of society, only so long as he provides service to the society. He deserves protection from physical assault in society, and preservation of his property; yet he has obligations to further the interests of society and his fellow citizens. These obligations include productive labor, which he can advance individually acting in the economy, or as service to the community. He may even extend a financial payment, in lieu of labor; if he possesses sufficient wealth. He can demand the Government protect him from adversity, but he must give equivalent labor in return.

8

Role of Government

Human interaction stands as the most intensive emotional arena of all endeavor. Reality expresses this area as exhortation where the cooperation of others can be obtained. Great emotion generates when this cooperation fails. Government, in it's function, serves as supervisory organ through which this human interaction may be conducted. Government serves as the forum for the debate and resolution of problems of the totality of society. It codifies a regulation of anti-social behavior; such activity fined, or otherwise punished, for the protection of the Individual in society. The conduct of Government, in addition, serves as an example of the pathway and common courtesy to be used in the resolution of private disputes. Deviant behavior on the part of Governmental leadership will soon filter down to common Citizens, setting the tone of individual relationships. The Government level, therefore, contains vital importance in the determination of Individual conduct inside society.

With the importance of Government comes an essential danger; levels of corruption are always highest in the ranks of Government, because it is here major dispersals of social advantage are found. The lowest rank and criminal always attempt to infest the Government and it's functionaries, in the furtherance of their own devious designs. Government officialdom should be picked for a proven ethical character; they are not. The term 'Politician' often hold rank lower than 'Lawyer'; both extreme in emotive contempt, though each should stand for high ideals. Reality explains the contempt; both occupations hold little interest for the layman, and lesser men only enter these occupations for the enrichment of their own fortunes. The Evil in society recognize these Individuals as prime candidates for corruption, while normal citizens doubt their leadership would act in such deplorable manner.

Social conditioning retards adequate social control of Government activities. Successful elements of society reached their positions, by utilization of the structure of society as existent. Government activity perceived as benign, if not beneficial. The success of the Individual seems justification for the activity of Government, it being the environment under which success was achieved. Change in Government procedure will be seen as a threat to the success attained. Less successful elements of society lack financial assets for endurance of conflict with corrupt Government functionaries, who are entrenched with support from both the source of corruption, and those who fear change as threat to their own success. Government control of the regulation of competition to attain individual success, ensures a complaint leadership of private centers of power; Individuals who are willing to deal with corrupt Governmental officialdom to maintain their own success. Government control of the Press comes easily with the conscription of the leadership of private industry, with control of Journalists hired and aired. Government officialdom can always pressure for the airing of their own viewpoint, even with a hostile Press. The desires of the citizenry becomes easily lost, with the advance of Government policy; also easily corrupted, through payments and benefits most easily generated by those willing to cheat their fellow citizens.

Another source of Governmental corruption comes from the sheer size of the population. Government alters as the numbers of the governed increase. Population enlargement engenders greater specialization of labor; said occupations developing their own social agenda. Politicians evolve into a professional class; building immunity from the desires of the citizenry, through personal associations with their fellow class elements. Normal citizens find it useless to eject Individuals from the political structure; professional politicians will prohibit anyone but those furthering their own agenda to stand for election, through the control of the electoral process. Individual politicians can be rejected because of obnoxious behavior, but the obnoxiousness of the political program cannot be displaced, through lack of viable alternative candidates with differing agenda. This professional class of Politicians seize greater entrenchment and power with turn to corrupt practice, where they receive heightened economic benefit.

The specialization of labor with increased population also determines the development of an additional level of insulation for Government function and corruption. Each specialized class of labor builds it's own form of political action, along with construction of their individual class political agenda. Each mutates into a specialized form of Lobbyist. Another layer is formed and interjected between common citizens and Government. Normal citizens, with their own desires for political action, lose personal access to their representatives; who will meet only with the Lobbyists–be they the representatives of occupational classes, or the front men of criminal elements in society. Normal citizens functionally suffer from political castration.

The only protection for the Individual under these political conditions lies in a clear outline of civil liberties and property rights; this only under intense pressure on the Courts to enforce such protections. The Courts, though, are staffed by officialdom nominated and appointed by the political officialdom, already differentiated into a professional political class, and highly subject to corruptive practice as mentioned above. Court officialdom, therefore, will be attuned to the political agenda of the Government. Their official performance will coincide with the desires of the political structure, unless normal citizens are united in their demand for observance of their civil liberties and property rights. Conditions for this universal demand of defense of civil liberties and property rights must be established, else normal citizens will still be left without protection. The most intrinsic need resides in the education of the populace. This education cannot be political exhortation; for in this case, it will be conscripted by the professional political class. They will substitute their own desires, in the stead of a real civil education of the people. Educational facilities and Press must be enjoined to provide such education as to the rights of the citizenry.

The first step to such education lies in the definition of the specific civil liberties and property rights of the Individual in society. Educational facilities must be compelled to compile a specific Paper of less than fifty pages, which clearly state what rights and protections are open to the Individual in society, along with the venues to assure recognition of those rights and protections. This Paper must be accepted by all scholars on the subject of civil liberties and property rights. The professional political class must be compelled to pass legislation mandating the teaching of this Paper to all students, in classes for students between 12-18 years of age. This can be done in a basic Civics course. The proposed law would also mandate each Newspaper and Magazine must publish some appropriate segment of this Paper in every issue, as element of the license to publish. Private and parochial schools, including home schooling, will not be exempt from the promulgation of this Paper; nor will religious Newspapers and Magazines escape publication of this Paper. The law will also stipulate the methodology by which this Paper will be updated, and the Paper will state clearly the reasons for the revision of the Paper.

An examination of the elements of such a Paper need be undertaken. The rights of the Individual when faced with law enforcement sanction must obviously be present. The property rights of the Individual must be sufficiently outlined, as the normal citizen can understand to what uses he can utilize his property. The Paper must clearly outline what uses a citizen, and especially business and industry, cannot make of his property; this a clear exposition of pollution controls and environmental hazards. The issue of Governmental impoundment of personal property must be explored, and the requirements for legitimate Government exercise of such power. The issue of Free Speech and Communication must be clearly assigned, with notification of all Government sanctions against such rights. A concise examination of Government Public Health controls must be made, with what legitimate powers can be exercised by the Government officialdom. The limitations of Government Police Power must be clearly stated, with precise statements of what law enforcement agents are empowered to do, and what they are not empowered to do. The Paper should finish with concise statements of what the Individual may do to others, and what he must not do; else be subject of criminal action by Government prosecutors.

The above-mentioned law must insist Teacher, Instructor, and Editor editorialize before and after such instruction; such efforts to insure the clear understanding of those receiving such awareness training. Such Individuals must not deviate from the essential intent of the Paper; content altered only to clarify. The Law must also stipulate Court officialdom must publish in local Newspapers in layman language, any deviation of decision from the basic rights as outlined by the approved Paper of dissemination. This lay publication must precisely state the exact cause of such deviation. Any deviation which is adopted for future universal application, must be included with it's relevant cause within a revised Paper for public dissemination. The precise educational intent will be maintained by law, for the proper education of citizenry.

Such a law or laws could be expanded to establish firmly the relationship between Church and State. History instructors throughout the primary and secondary grades could be impelled to teach all basic tenants of each individual religion operative in the Nation. A manual could be prepared by Educators, a compilation of data gathered from each religious leadership which has been approved by a Committee of religious leaders of all religions within the Nation. All Schools would be compelled to teach from this manual, even parochial schools dedicated to one religion. The laws garner expansion with limitations set upon all religions, in order to maintain their ability to function as a religious organization. No religion would be allowed to preach against any other religion; no religion would be allowed to attack any group of

Individuals, associations, or cultural styles allowed by law, through any public or written pronouncements; no religion would be allowed to advocate racial or cultural hatred, condemn sexual preferences of anyone unaffiliated with their religion, or criticize the cultural preferences of other citizens of the Nation. Violation of this law would lead to loss of tax immunity, injunction against such religious leadership from preaching or educating children, and injunction from advertising or using public airways (including Internet and telecommunications) to preach their message of hatred. The Law should stipulate all religions must pay the same tax as secular business, if such religions engage in marketing and production of secular or religious products. A final element to the Law could be refusal to allow any but approved clergy to live on religious property; this to insure no physical or mental deprivation techniques are used for brainwashing purpose, and to guarantee all private citizens pay their fair share of tax. Religions in violation of the above elements of the proposed law, could be charge with Cultural Assault; the charge stipulated to be the equivalent of Physical Assault on a Person, with the same personal punishments for the Violators. Religion, while condoned and shared by almost all citizens, will also be subject to control by Law.

Many will claim such codification would bring endangerment to freedom of religion. This is not the intent of this Author, or any proposed legislation. Understanding must reach all that religious congregations and clergy must submit to the same restrictions from aberrant behavior, as do private citizens. Legislation would guarantee a cultural matrix where all could live according to their beliefs in safety. Failure to clearly define the role of religion in society, will always lead to religious transgressions out of fervor; their cultural neighbors are always the ones who suffer. This stands as unacceptable in a Time where Science has provided the wherewithal for even private citizens to produce massive destruction.

The nature of Government, itself, must change; unless the Sins of the Past be revisited upon all of the World. There exists a vast bureaucratic calcification of all Government structure; brought on by development of the above-mentioned professional Politician class, along with the creation of the occupational class of Civil Servants. The upshot of the power of these two occupational classes operating in conjunction, curtails any innovation within Governmental structure. These classes expanded their power and influence inside the old Government structure, and all new measures must satisfy the necessities of maintenance of that power and influence. Efficiency is functionally discarded, solely because it would challenge the foundations upon which these classes rest.

Most citizens do not realize the danger of this intransigence, yet is far deadlier to human liberty than any other factor. Governmental functionaries will amend any right of any citizen, in maintenance of this power and influence. A prime example is the allocation of Social Security Disability benefits. A Citizen cannot acquire any benefits by direct petition to the Government administration; he is always denied, and told to get a lawyer. The sole rationale being Civil Service administration can determine the level of benefits, without suffering the complaints of the actual Petitioner. The insistence on the acquirement of legal representation insists on a legal determination of benefit award, where the Civil Service already has a functioning relationship with the Court; itself staffed by professional Civil Service personnel. It is the complete silencing of the political voice of private citizens!

The wants, needs, and desires of the private citizenry will always be silenced by the interaction of professional Politicians and professional Civil Servants; who are committed to the status quo, under which their power was developed. Another prime example of deep threat to citizenry comes in the form of simple denial of Habeas Corpus by the Government, subsequent to the Terrorist attacks. Government Civil Servants simply prevailed on the Civil Servants employed as legal clerks of the Court system, to reject acceptance of such petitions. They refuse to place such writs in the Court schedule. The writ of Habeas Corpus is specifically defined in the Constitution of the United States, yet an entrenched Civil Service can and does refuse to act upon such applications, though they are compelled by Oath and Law to do so.

Many now claim it is a period of National Emergency; such divergences are compelled for Security reasons. Reality persists in the explanation such activities do not increase the security of Americans, who are still in as great a danger as they were on September 11th, 2001. It continues to state almost all held Individuals have been proven to possess no Terrorist connections. They are still held, because Civil Service functionaries find it easier to catalogue foreign immigrants in this Country, by intense interrogation of the confined Individuals. The Civil Servants conducting these interrogations, which are illegal without evidence of personal crime, solely because they have not been served with a Writ of Habeas Corpus. It is patent False Imprisonment, a violation of the United States Constitution, and legalized by no Court. It remains a repetition of incarceration of Innocents on the order of the Japanese-Americans of World War II, and done as it was; unlawful orders given by Politicians and Civil Servants acting in violation to American law.

The United States citizen still enjoys greater protection from his own Government, than does the citizen of Nations where Terrorist organizations found and grow. Law in such Nations stands as what a Government functionary defines it to be; a victimized citizen must find a superior Government functionary who is sympathetic (usually for a financial fee), to free himself from Government persecution. Americans, therefore, fail to respond to danger signs to their liberty. Civil Service generates regulations continually, which encroach upon their daily lives. Corruption insures this regulation is often to the advantage of business interests. A minor example can amplify the tremendous impact of this regulation. Giant Retail Grocery chains find it much simpler to sell frozen Beef Liver, than fresh Beef Liver. The unfrozen Beef Liver must be sold within ten days, and transporting unfrozen Meat from Processing Plants require special storage with enhanced cost. Small Grocery stores, butchering locally, sold ninety percent of the Beef Liver; which is much better fresh than frozen. Unfrozen Beef Liver cannot be sold anywhere today by Civil Service regulation; at least, in the Author's home State. It is an incredibly minor note, but an excellent expression of Civil Service constriction of American life by regulation; it is estimated there are Ten millions Civil Service regulations currently on the books in the United States, all affect some aspect of American life. Maybe one hundred thousand such regulations serve the interests of the average American.

The power of the professional Politician class, the professional Civil Service class, and the Special Interests which corrupt them, must be challenged. Americans are losing personal choice every day. Americans must buy automobiles with Safety belts and Air bags, though the rate of injuries per accident have not decreased from the era of automobiles without them; the reason being the increasing flimsiness of current automobile construction. Such measures have simply kept the statistics from worsening, at Manufacturers' ability to charge a 700 percent markup for these features. An integrated Roll-bar Cage has not been introduced to automobile regulation, because Manufacturers' could not easily pass on such cost to the Consumer. It is the Author's estimation such a Cage would cost less than the current markup price for Safety Belts and Air Bags. Accident injuries could be cut in half, with the use of both integrated Roll-bar Cage and Safety Belts with Air Bags. It becomes clear by such example, Civil Service regulation does not have Personal protection as the end-goal of their endeavors. A reversion to the previous example of fresh Beef Liver could state there have been fewer cases of Food Poisoning from eating fresh Beef Liver, in the entire history of the United States; than cases of Food Poisoning from Fast Food Chains any Two year period, since the inauguration of such Restaurants. There is still little adequate Civil Service regulation of Fast Food handling of Food, Food preparation, or training of such Restaurant personnel. Civil Service regulation serves the purpose of Those who pay for it. Americans must break the vicious cycle, which remains more harmful than beneficial.

One appropriate method to break the power of the Civil Service could be elimination of entrenched structure of the organization. Civil Servants embed themselves with high retirement benefits, high seniority pay, and safety from discharge from service, no matter the quality of their labor. Attack on this intransigence may be made by fundamental alteration of the Civil Service, on a pattern organized for Military service. The first element to the Plan would be the creation of an effective Draft law. The Draft legislation would expound the principle all Government service derives all personnel from a universal draft; no one to be subject to more than Six years' service per lifetime. All citizens would be subject to draft between the ages of 18-55. The term of Six years determined by one year of apprenticeship training, and five years of qualified service. Government draft boards would determine if draftees would be assigned to Military or Civil Service; also decide if a Civil Service selectee would be detailed to Federal, State, or Local service. State and Local Government pay the Federal Government for the training of Civil Servants, based on pro-rated hourly wage scales. Employees under the old Civil Service program allowed to continue their employment under the old terms of service, not to exceed a period of twenty years after the implementation of the universal draft law.

The quantity of power expressed by the Civil Service broken by the inability of Individual application for position, the qualitites of power can also be broken by simple measures. Civil Service shall be limited to Six years, unless a certain Rank is attained, at which the time of service can be doubled to Twelve years; never to be exceeded, except at the behest of National Security, and never to extend beyond the current elected Federal administration. This measure would insure no one could make Civil Service employment a lifetime employment. Rank would imitate Military Service, and solely determine continuance beyond Six years. Attainment of Rank would automatically dictate transfer to an alternate level of Government, say from Federal to State, or Local to Federal. This measure forestalls extended personal entrenchment in departmental position, as well as eliminating personal aggrandizement by Level employment (Federal employees could not claim superiority over Local and State employees). Draftees will be chosen for their capabilities and specialties, and assigned entry Rank by the Draft board or agency. This utilizes personal success achieved in the Private sector for Government service; it also generates innate desire for return to Private employment.

Pay Scale will be used to destroy the basic potential entrenchment of the Civil Service. Both Military and Civil Service will be paid at an effective 70% of Private sector pay for equivalent occupation. This can be justified, by insistence all Military and Civil Service personnel live in Government-owned housing assigned by Rank. This will cut great Government expense in maintenance of Government personnel, plus eliminate the primary capital aggregation method of American households–the ownership of housing. The advantage of Civil Service has been eliminated; it is no longer a programable method to attain a successful standard of living. Civil Servants feel compelled to leave Civil Service at the point possible, to build a viable financial posture. The length of terms of Service are sufficiently short, as to provide no threat to the ability of building a successful financial posture for Individuals; with experience in Government service providing good job resumes for future employment. The restriction to Government housing for Military and Civil Servants will eliminate personal prestige assertions, as well as cancel objections to transfer.

Incentives to get Civil Servant draftees to engage in hard labor will be attained by the issuance of the equivalent of 'Honorable Discharge', currently used by the Military. Such an 'Honorable Discharge' from either Military or Civil Service will grant a 25% increase of Social Security benefit upon retirement for Six years' service, or 50% increase of such benefit upon Twelve years' service. This measure assures desire for an 'Honorable Discharge', such discharges can be set up as based upon accomplishment during Service on a Point system, and success in Private employment highly desired because low Pay scales in Service provide low Social Security benefit levels. Civil and Military Service becomes desirable because of long-term potential benefits, while continuous employment in the Public Sector leads to personal disadvantage.

Civil Service will be altered in nature, so all current regulators will be faced with the regulations later in life, which they now implement and enforce. Their willingness to work with Small Business and Private Individuals will increase, along with their response to complaints from common citizens. They come to realize rigid enforcement past good sense pays them nothing, and brings down-the-road difficulties to themselves. Corruption pays little in the long-run for them as Individuals; and positional power will alter with promotion, coming with hard work on their part—to maintain their Points for 'Honorable Discharge'. The long-term gain for their efforts come from later success in the Private Sector. Civil Servants will finally actually function as Servants of the Public.

The limitation of the power of the professional Politicians will be much harder to curtail, due to opportunity of all citizens to engage in the Political process. A primary change in Election law could insist each Candidate file a Public Position Paper with the Election Committee, outlining the specific outline of their proposed administration of the Office sought; to be published before the Election. Another possibility lie in the demand each Candidate publish the list of Political appointees he will make to Government position, before the date of the Election. A third option is the passage of legislation insisting Political appointees to Government office pass a Two-hour written examination on the understanding of the parameters of the office, along with an Oral Board of Academics expert on the history of the office. The written examination which must be passed with a score of Eighty would assure the Appointee had knowledge of the responsibility of the office. The Oral Boards would assure the Appointee had knowledge of the limitation of power of the office, and awareness of the dangers of misuse of the powers of office. Passage of the Oral Board requiring an average of 70 of the three middle scores of a Five-member Oral Board. Political candidates must publish their Political Appointees along with their scores from the written examination and Oral Boards prior to the Election.

The change would be extremely minor in the short-term from such measures, with the current employment of highly competent staffs. The long-terms consequences may hold much greater benefit, as Press begins to equate Test scores with later performance. Political candidates would find increasing pressure to nominate Appointees with a intimate knowledge of the positions filled. Professional Politicians feeling pressure to specialize, the number of positions they could fill would be vastly reduced. It would no longer be a question of on-the-job training for either the Appointee or the Candidate. They would be compelled to learn the parameters of the offices sought, prior to the seeking. There remains fewer offices which they could seek, and greater fear of being replaced by an irrate Public. The overall effect may be higher performance, in terms of benefit for the Public.

9

The Leadership Roll

The delineation of leadership remains a difficult task, but the Press contains the best possibility for proper selection of leadership. The Press holds little benefit under it's current mode of operation, though change of methodology presents high relevance for the presentation of proper leadership. Present concentration on the immediacy of events castrates the Press as an effective force in society. The Public gains small insight by simple 'Who did what' relation of fact. The discussion becomes disjointed segments of meaningless gossip. Focus on sensationalism breeds drift away from constructive analog. The current matrix among the Press Corps defeats the proclaimed desire of the Press, which is the enlightenment of the Public as to current events.

The traditional Press questions of 'Who', 'What', 'Why', 'When', and 'How', must be supplemented by more decisive questions, in order for the Public to make relevant use of the information. "Who' need to be extended to 'Who is this Individual, what is his prior history, is his current action in accordance with prior exhibited behavior, does his life history predict this type of behavior?'. 'What' must expand to "What is this action or behavior, how does it differentiate from the normal procedure, is this a violation of current practice, and what consequences could such deviation possess?'. 'Why' becomes 'Why is this Event important, who is it going to impact along with how such impact may occur, does this Event predict a recurrence of similar activity, and if so, what possible consequence will incur?'. 'When' expands to 'Where in the concourse of human events did this activity occur, what prior indications of such events were present, is there a predictable frequency to these events, and what possible options are available to forestall or impel recurrence?' 'How' turns into 'What circumstances brought on this activity, could those circumstances be replicated or hindered, what failure of responsibility or success of endeavor created these events?'. The bottom line insists the Journalist stands as a social eunuch, if he is not first a Historian.

Journalism cannot serve any function, without the definition of leadership. It need present this leadership for ability to forecast a foreseeable outcome, i.e., the prediction of forecasts. Lack of forecasting eliminates durable reader or viewer response, because of no conceptional issuance of impact. The end-user can find no rationale for reading or viewing, except for entertainment. Direction of human social movement lifts Journalism from simple entertainment; the definition of leadership outlines the basic social movement. Trouble arises as Journalism holds no great success record in the defining of new leadership. This entails through the insufficiency of methodology used by the Media.

Research holds the prime refuge for the Journalist. It possesses protection from charges of Libel and Slander. It carries the shield of certified truth. It brings the source of new stories. It defends against charges of misrepresentation. It sustains continued investigation. It creates a thirst in readership for more information. It contains the foundation for all reportage. It fails only in it's lack of use! The Journalist fails in definition of leadership, through failure to research and publish results.

Every potential leadership cadre, whether Political, Social, Religious, Educational, or other should have a pre-Death obituary constructed and published; it should contain his accomplishments, his failures, his previous impact on his fellow citizenry, his position on the most important issues of the Period, his Plans for the future, and his personal conduct towards others—family, friends, co-workers, subordinates, and ethnic groups. His beliefs should be outlined, along with exhibited willingness to accept the beliefs of others, most especially those whose beliefs conflict with his own. Reader and Viewer should be presented with a total construct method to judge the worth of the Individual.

The reviewed leadership examined for the temperance and balance of his belief system; the complex evaluated for potential danger of targeted ways of life. Analysis of personal associations and membership in organizations detailed in any radical or socially unresponsive venues expressed in prior operation. The nature of his support studied for reliability of continued support, the nature and content of that support investigated for violations of individual rights of citizens or groups, and the true source of financial support discerned. Each story done on each leadership cadre should contain some rational exposition of this research. The total culmination of stories on the Individual needs to give the audience a clear image of the Individual in all his aspects.

◆   ◆   ◆

Turn must finally be made to examination of the Leadership role itself. The first aspect detailed contains the thought Leadership roles evolve, based upon the size of the population of the lead. Leadership must acquire Management skills, simply because the largesse of their followers increase. The Concept seems clear in construct, but entails great difficulty in action. The Population of the World reaches incredible levels; the number of human Souls ever to have lived on this World prior to 1900 (all generations), was exceeded by the living Population not of Today, but of 1960; it is twice as large Today. The expansion of Communications within the last Twenty years has tripled. All Leadership suffers from rapid growth as awareness extends to vast numbers of potential followers. Almost all organic Leadership fails, as their Movement expands beyond their capacity to lead.

The above fact creates the reality People lack Leadership, under the intense pressure of rapid Population expansion. Traditional leadership organizations fail the test of Leadership; their procedural rules were developed for a greatly lesser following, and committed to programs adequate for followings of size under which those procedural rules generated. Such organizations reorganize to protect the policies accepted, and turn in Sectarian doctrinarians. They do not fulfil the needs of their followers, and use their power to forestall development of sounder Leadership. They lose the support of their following; maintaining power solely because of the lack of alternative leadership existent. Excellent examples of this failure can be found in the Democratic and Republican Parties in the United States. Reaganomics was obsolete before it was introduced in the early 1980s, and still espoused by most of the Party organization Today. The Democratic Party is in even worse shape, spouting the ideals of FDR and Kennedy.

Other alternatives for Leadership structure follow Sectarian outlines, boasting of programs even older than the current Leadership structural organization. AFL-CIO, NAACP, ACCLU, or Born-Again Christians, each and all possess obsolescence professing an ideology for a much smaller, less complex society. The David Karishs' and the Aryan Brotherhood recognize this fact, while the previous organizations do not. All of the organizations operate effectively only so long as their following is structurally limited; none of their ideological programs will work, as they are not actually alone on this World.

Functional Leadership organizations will only succeed when Educational practices are unified. Only when the greatest segment of the World Population enjoys a common Educational base, does effective structural Leadership have chance to develop. Failure to provide this universal similarity of Education will bring only Enclave leadership, even at the National and Regional level. The Internet ensures cross-pollination of ideals, with constant comparison of all program ideology. Exponents face organic opposition to almost every program element; instead of evolving their program, they retreat into an extreme Sectarian base unacceptable to the rest of the World. This totally destroyed their Leadership capacity.

The first resolution new Leadership must accept is the impossibility of limiting outside influence; the outside Population numbers along with their productivity, preclude such exclusion. The Taliban forbade TV, Radio, and Internet access on pain of death; they received American bombs and troops. Current Afghanis need vast foreign aid to feed themselves; this would have been the case, even with Taliban maintenance of power, due to drought conditions with the nation. This reflects current economic interaction, now so great no nation can withdraw without a huge reduction in the standard of living for the people of that nation. No one can survive without cooperation with culturally differentiated elements contrary to one's own social system. New Leadership must understand the Polity has expanded beyond any national borders, or any religious belief system.

The next recognition of new Leadership comes in the establishment of policy based upon at least passive acceptance of the total World polity. Anything less will limit expansion to a specific segment, with much less influence and power expressible Today, than in periods of less cross-pollination. Programs cannot succeed with messages of racial, religious, or cultural discrimination. Any Program, even the most innocuous, will almost immediately suffer Hate attacks from Sectarian formations. No Program will survive without ability to persuade the total Polity these Hate attacks are unjustified. Failure to do this brings rapid de-escalation of support for the Program. Criticism has to be silenced, almost impossible, or shown as discriminatory; the alternative will be Sectarian propaganda succeeds.

The third element adopted must be development of expandable Policies. Anything proposed, or made in organizational program, has to have the ability of expansion through all cultural conditioning. Leadership favoring a certain class, culture, or population segment finds immediate curtailment of options; such programs will not penetrate the present cultural mix. This will again change with a substantive increase in Population levels, as more cultural segments realize Sectarian policy becomes necessary for protection of property and capital. This retreat, though, holds no benefit; being a form of regional 'thuggee-ism'. Responsible Leadership devise programs of unity.

The last element of Leadership mandatory with the increasing access consists of the development of a total cultural identity. The spread of Sectarianism through the World in the past decades comes from inability of old cultural values to meet modern population pressures. The inclusive cultural identity offered by older leadership systems fail to encompass all the needs of Individuals today. The Individual cannot work within the society he needs to work within, and meet the obligations of older espoused cultural systems. This remains the primary root cause of Terrorism. The Individual becomes faced with two alternatives: abandon the modern society he is in, and retreat into some mythical idyllic realm; or surrender the cultural values under which he was raised. The first produces Sectarianism and Terrorism, the second leaves the Individual rootless and isolated from security. New Leadership has to provide a security-blanket of cultural values consistent with the values under which the Individual was raised, but also capable with dealing with the quandaries of modern life.

The conditions of Leadership also change in the new matrix of communications. Future Leadership will have to Post daily discussion of the Internet, open and free to all debate. Nothing else can satisfy a Polity dedicated to knowing the minutia of daily operation. This Leadership, or their writers, must be able to debate in Print; the debates set by the questions asked, avoidance will be perceived as deception. The operation will reverse the fundamental caveat of propaganda or Public Relations; this consisting of always setting the agenda. Spin-doctoring does not transfer well to the Internet. Leadership planning will alter from yesteryear; the modern Leader must concentrate on policy formation, rather than ad-hoc executive operation. A justification for every action will be the watchword; failure will bring immediate loss of support. An elected official will spend Six months in intense debate on the Internet, else he will fail election within a decade. Internet Discussion Forum captures the sentiment of a Polity increasingly driven to involvement greater than spaced elections.

Political pressure already builds for an electronic Newsletter created daily, giving discussion of Organizational activity. Hidden Civil Servants who today dictate the lifestyle of Millions of peoples, will soon discover strident demands for daily reports from those peoples; who will be so insistent, they must know the names of the Civil Servants' wives and children, previous jobs held, an electronic image to curse, and the method of their employment. The demands do not stop at the personal; they will want a spreadsheet outline of current operations, what Mandates the operations are being conducted under, the progress being made, and the cost of said operations in Accountant formulation. Current Politicians proclaim no one but Crackpots would desire this information; but such Web sites will generate Millions of hits per month. This will prove true for any level of Government, once the children using the Computer since Pre-School attain Voting Age.

Journalism will alter with this new Polity as well. Computer tracking becomes the new research tool. Another decade will witness Journalists able to determine the exact expenditure of a Government department to the last dollar, without access to Government accounts. They will track the daily activity of any Employee of Government through his credit card slips, unless they determine the Employee is withdrawing heavy amounts of cash from his accounts; not through his bank records, but through purchase recording. The new Journalists will possess more accurate financial records on any Politician, than Credit companies today provide for potential Lenders. Untoward financial expenditures by any Government functionary, or heavy Contributor to Political campaigns, will soon be read about in the daily news. The technology implicit in Hacker technology today, will assure Journalists' ability to track every dollar spent in the World, within a Score of Years.

The Leader of the future should know any payment made to or by himself will be Public knowledge. He will not be able to live in a house he could not have paid for; Journalists will spot the excess expenditure. He must report all Employees and Supporters, else read about them in the News or on the Internet. Contributions are reported, or tracked from Source to end-deposit. A dozen years will allow for Journalist reportage of total largesse of Tips per year, and to who; excessive Tipping, or the failure to Tip properly, could cost a political Candidate an election. Journalists may be in the employ of Power brokers, in the capacity of Spin-doctors, yet nothing will stop the Hackers on the Internet. There are three Programs today, which track better than the Federal Reserve's internal accounts. One can track every check, real or electronic, issued by the U.S. Treasury in the World. Eleven Hackers have currently been jailed, for downloading the complete bank records of a major institutional bank; they did not even steal any money. All financial records will soon be Public, the Leader of the future cannot escape.

There is currently a Whistle-blowing debacle about falsification of quality-control data for batteries in guidance control for weapons; failures of these guidance systems are said to have killed Americans in Afghanistan. Whistle-blowing will become a daily pastime in the future, with simple Post to the Internet with data. Employers must fear for their lives if they act unethically, or pay whatever pay raises every employee demands. A friend has suggested the Author moderate a Industrial Malfeasance Forum; to be met with the suggestion the job would be a full-time occupation, with necessary added staff. The time it takes for an unethical action on the part of some organization to surface, will reduce from years to weeks under the impact of Internet tracking and reportage. No one, especially political Leaders, can find protection.

The final aspect of Leadership altered by the new reality comes in the form of inability to escape the Past. Previous position will brand for life! Anything known by anyone will reach the electronic page, if not Newsprint. Failed policy must always be explained, if not defended. Future Leaders must become a family friend, then never betray that trust. Deception already lies as the greatest Crime, worse than adultery or bribery; because of the complexity of modern existence; everyone must integrate dozens of facts per day, utterly disrupting the schedule if proven to be false datum introduced. Deliberate introduction of false datum, for whatever reason, incurs utter condemnation. Friendships built on telephone lines, cannot endure lies. Leadership must realize they cannot be caught in a lie; all will abandon them.

10

Conclusion

This Work found original scope as examination of Philosophical commentary on the practice of Terrorism. Mutation came early, as realization arrived such a Study would require a vast amount of research best conducted by Seminar team. The Author was quickly dissuaded from the beginning intent, through lack of investigative assistance. He felt the Reader need not review the propagandist tirades of Marx, Lenin, Trotsky, Bucharinn, and the early Twentieth Century Anarchists of Spain, to comprehend the nature of Terrorism. More conventional Authors discuss Terrorism only in a disjoint manner, and require hundreds of hours of research to dramatize their condemnation of Terrorism. The Author reverted to relation of his own homilies in this project. Suffice it to say condemnation of Terrorism does exist in philosophical literature, especially in the writings of Montesque and Rabin.

Terrorism has been discussed to some degree, as to it's subordination of the Individual to an Ideal, the conditions under which it's generates advocates, and it's outpouring from the development of Sectarianism. Some methods have been advanced on effective ideological contest with the ideological set. This in no manner provides a definitive plan to control the gross destruction of Terrorists and their organizations. This is the periphery of Law Enforcement, who are far more able to advance proper modes of operation. It should be mentioned these efforts can only be measured in degrees of effectiveness, and Terrorist organizations need only one instance out of hundreds of attempts to garner success.

The Author herein states firmly only the advent of Universal Education will reduce the incidence of Terrorism. The instillation of common values among all participants on this World, holds the only constraint of Terrorism. Understand Corruption as the propellent used by all Terrorist propaganda, to gain advocates of violence. Until Governments and Societies cease the use of violence to further personal-gain agendas, little headway will be made against oppositionist terrorism. The Author does not advocate an end of warfare; such swill is foolhardy, and refuses to recognize the fundamental animal nature of the human soul. Warfare exists because Individuals believe they can profit by the destruction of others, and the needs of others to defend from such people. Proposal of Utopias will not bring Peace to humanity; only successful personal defense brings the desired condition.

The most successful actual venue for combating Terror comes in the use of Assassination and the issuance of Bounties on known Terrorists. Two efforts operate against the consistent use of this asset. The first opposition resides in Political leadership, who possess real fears of this system being used against themselves. The second opposition resides in the screams of supporters of Terrorists, said screams so adequately reported by Journalists. The fact stands Anyone who publicly calls for the death of others by violence, should face similar liability. The old Humanitarian call for better conduct than expressed by those advocating violence, should be dismissed as foolish in the midst of Innocents dying. It holds no expression of civilized conduct, allowing known murderers to continue their attacks. The Author admits to a partisanship for such activity, along with no dedication to current political or social leadership.

Any defense must be based upon consistent threat, inconsistency or lack of threat provides opportunity to those willing to destroy the lives of others for personal gain. It would be nice for a society to live by God's Word; yet, it contains the seeds of Suicide. Amiable resolution of Conflict issues in the face of one Participant willing to use violence, holds no effective element except to drain determination from some

Participants. Negotiation demands desire for Peace among all involved; all Terrorist organizations and the societies which spawn them, derive their power from violence. They will not abandon the avenue of their original success. United States tries to broker an agreement between Israel and the PLO, a stupidity because of the creation of both entities; an acceptable treaty for One, will never be acceptable to the Other, because of their basic differences joined with willingness to attack. The only end to the violence in the area, will come from the clear ascendency of power by one or the other. This stipulates a consistency of threat produced by one side.

The growth of Sectarianism in the World highlights only one factor, there are failing societies and cultures. Rational thought states these cultures will adapt for survival, or die. Further evaluation equates only the Youth of these cultures as capable of the adaptability. End of conflict will come only with the death of these cultures, in their present form. Expectation of survival for older elements in all cultures fails to capture the essence of life, which is change. Our Forebears could not live in Our society; We survived only because We adapted and evolved from what they were and could do. Failing cultures will survive only if they adapt, this by a process of component death among their current makeup. Sectarianism with it's residue of violence will not abate, until this process is significantly complete. Lack of educational input from successful cultures will delay this process, and prolong the violence associated with it.

The real threat of Terrorism comes from the uneven transference of this educational input. More advanced elements of failing cultures possess advanced contacts with failing elements of their culture. It is consistent with Our realization that Our Parents are mortal, and will someday die. The threat of Terrorism comes from this phenomena; more advanced elements believing they can relieve pressure on the failing elements of their culture, by attacking the more successful cultures from which they have learned. Terrorists fail to realize their own adaption provides equal pressure on the failing elements of their own culture, they are as much the Agent of Death as are successful cultures. Age and Incompetence determines what fails, not the activity of successful cultures. The Terrorists need more advanced education, not just the Young of failing cultures.

Will We survive the wave of Terrorism? The answer is Yes. Every culture and society faces it's own matrix of strife; itself in flux, and altering with the development of the culture. The strife will increase in degree of development and trouble, until such time as Our culture will also start to fail; said failure the result of Our own incompetence in handling the World, at the time of the failure. We are far from that point, due to the complex of resources at Our command. We have to accept the fact the World in which We were spawned, will not be the World in which We will die as a culture. We are still expanding as a culture, introducing new concepts and practices; We have not yet stopped the deaths of Our own Parents, and never will. We enjoy leadership in the World today, but must understand We cannot stop the death around Us. It retains the essence of it's own being; and will end as it fails. We must go on, produce what We can; failure our Future, but not now!